SUPERIOR HIKING TRAIL GUIDEBOOK

The official resource for Minnesota's premier natural footpath

NINTH EDITION

Produced by the **SUPERIOR HIKING TRAIL ASSOCIATION**

The Superior Hiking Trail®

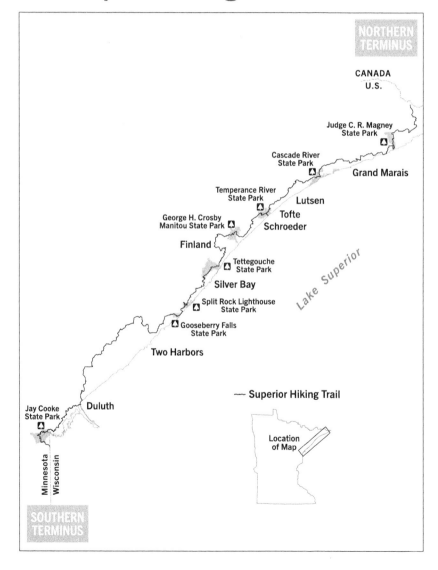

Superior Hiking Trail Guidebook

Printed in the United States of America by Bang Printing

Cover and text design: Sally Rauschenfels
Map illustrations: Matt Kania, Map Hero Inc.
Cover photo: John Schwager
Cover photo location: Lookout Mountain

Although the Superior Hiking Trail Association has researched all sources to ensure the accuracy and completeness of the information contained in this book, we assume no responsibility for errors, inaccuracies, omissions, or any inconsistency herein. Information is current as of the date of publication.

ISBN: 978-1-7343175-3-4

10 9 8 7 6 5 4 3 2 1

"The Superior Hiking Trail beckons us to experience the rugged landscape and natural communities of the North Shore. From ancient lava flows underfoot, stately white pine groves, tumbling cascades, the brilliant fall colors of old hardwood forests and delicate spring wildflowers to breathtaking vistas, the SHT offers soul-refreshing access to this priceless and unique region."

ı John Green, Former Superior Hiking Trail Association Board Member (1987-2013)

"The Superior Hiking Trail is much more than a footpath; it is a gateway to peace and inspiration for those who experience its rugged beauty. And whether it's just a few quiet hours or a long through-hike, spending time on the trail can awaken a conservation ethic within us, sending us home with a new sense of purpose to care for the natural world around us—no matter where we live."

ı Kris Larson, Minnesota Land Trust

"The Superior Hiking Trail is a Minnesota gem. There are multiple access points from south of Duluth to the Canadian border which lead you to incredible vistas."

ı Nancy Odden, Former Superior Hiking Trail Association Executive Director (1997-2001)

"The Superior Hiking Trail is one of our state's most treasured attractions, enjoyed by travelers from all over the world. Part of the expansive North Country National Scenic Trail, the SHT offers unparalleled views of great Lake Superior and the rugged shoreline along the way. The Trail is great for short day hikers taking a road trip up the North Shore "All-American Road," as well as backpack camping for ambitious hikers."

ı Alyssa Hayes, Explore Minnesota

"The Superior Hiking Trail is about connection. Connection with our natural world. Connection with that quiet place within ourselves. Connection with others; whether it be at a trail volunteer project, at an organized event on the trail or in that brief exchange as you pass another trail person going by."

ı John Storkamp, Rocksteady Running

Since 1993, the Superior Hiking Trail Association has published the *Guide to the Superior Hiking Trail* as the primary guidebook for the Trail. Eight editions of this guide have served the Association and thousands of SHT users well over the years, and we extend our appreciation to everyone who has contributed to those previous editions. In response to feedback from trail users, we've taken the opportunity to revisit and refresh how we present information about the Trail in the Ninth Edition to ensure it remains relevant and useful for today's SHT explorer. We've also updated the name to *Superior Hiking Trail Guidebook* to align with industry standards. ⋀⋀

Contents

Notice to Superior Hiking Trail Users

The information in this Guidebook has been collected, verified, and presented to you in the spirit of providing the most accurate data possible at the time of printing. However, the route of the Superior Hiking Trail and the locations of our trailheads and campsites are constantly evolving due to regular maintenance work, reroutes to improve the trail user experience, and the changing priorities of public and private landowners.

Please be aware: by the time you read this, some of the information included in this publication may no longer be accurate. Always follow on-the-ground signage over the information you see presented in this book. You can find more up-to-date information on changes to the Trail, conditions, and errata at superiorhiking.org.

The Superior Hiking Trail Association is dedicated to providing useful and accurate information to users of the Trail. If you have questions or concerns, please contact the Association in writing at PO Box 315, Two Harbors, MN 55616-0315, by phone at (218) 834-2700, or by email at info@superiorhiking.org. ⋏⋏

Past, Present, and Future of the Superior Hiking Trail Association

HOW THE TRAIL AND ASSOCIATION CAME TO BE

The concept for the Superior Hiking Trail was born out of a feasibility study put together by the U.S. Forest Service in the mid-1980s. The rugged, challenging landscape of the Sawtooth Mountains and the presence of Lake Superior offered an opportunity to experience the most spectacular vistas in the Midwest. With foresight, a dusting of destiny, and several critical investments, a group of visionaries—including federal, state, and local land managers; resort and business owners; and recreation enthusiasts—stepped up, often as volunteers, to build what would become the state's premier natural footpath along Lake Superior's North Shore.

The nonprofit Superior Hiking Trail Association was established in 1986 to lead the efforts to build, maintain, manage, and promote the Trail. The organization was made up of volunteers in the early days and eventually added staff to increase the organization's capacity as trail construction picked up pace. Over the years, many hands have made light work of building and maintaining the Trail, with considerable contributions from volunteers, contractors, agency partners, and trail supporters.

In 2019, the Superior Hiking Trail became an official part of the North Country National Scenic Trail (NCT). The SHT is a critical connection in the 5,000-mile route from Vermont to North Dakota, a national trail administered by the North Country Trail Association. When traversing the SHT, one is also on the NCT. The Superior Hiking Trail retains its own identity and will continue to be maintained and managed by the SHTA.

THE SHTA OF TODAY AND TOMORROW

As the Trail was constructed over decades, the Association has grown and adapted its operations to evolve with the Trail. With a route in place today, the focus of the organization has turned to protecting and renewing the Trail to ensure its corridor is secured and improved for future generations to enjoy.

The Association's operations are guided by a volunteer board of directors and managed by a small team of professional staff who work to improve the SHT experience and strive to connect the aspirations of those who use the Trail with those who care for the land. The Association leads the charge by harnessing the power of volunteers, supporters, agency partners, and trail users to break down barriers, engage participants, and create deeper relationships between people and nature.

As use of the Trail has increased, so have the Association's efforts to protect the natural landscapes along the Trail, engage users in stewardship of the Trail, educate visitors to minimize their impact, and preserve the experience so it can be enjoyed for decades to come. A few strategic focuses of the Association's work include:

Trail Protection. The most important behind-the-scenes work of the Association is assuring that there continues to be a Superior Hiking Trail. With over 200 private landowners and public land managers, the Association works to assure continued access to the Trail corridor through partnerships, easements, and other protective agreements. Without this work, there would be no Trail.

Sustainable Trail Building and Maintenance. Hundreds of volunteers and several trail maintenance contractors work tirelessly to maintain the Superior Hiking Trail, but many aging sections are in need of more technical renewal and improvement. Launched in 2018, the Association's Trail Renewal Program has focused on efforts to address problems on specific sections of the Trail, many of which are over 35 years old. These efforts include repairs, reroutes, new infrastructure, and other enhancements.

Education and Engagement. Every year the Association provides assistance to thousands of people to access, navigate, and enjoy the Trail responsibly. In addition, the Association has launched several efforts aimed at resolving visitor use management-related issues. A comprehensive website, publications like maps and guidebooks, signage, and events on and off the Trail help to educate SHT users. In addition to its own efforts, the Association relies on partnerships with other organizations to engage new and experienced users with educational resources to increase stewardship of the Trail.

Funding and Financial Sustainability. While the Trail is free to use, it requires considerable financial resources to manage. The Association uses multiple revenue sources to provide sustainable funding to protect and renew the Trail and educate Trail users. Funding sources include fundraisers, estate gifts, donor appeals, business sponsorships, and membership dues; state, federal, and foundation grants; and sales of goods through the SHTA's retail store. The Association is also the beneficiary of a long-term endowment fund at the Duluth-Superior Area Community Foundation.

Equity, Diversity, and Inclusion. Ensuring the Trail is a welcoming and inclusive outdoor recreation space for all users is a priority for the Association. The SHTA aims to develop a greater understanding of the history of the lands that the Trail crosses, and it has committed to ensure equity and inclusion are holistically integrated into the organization's culture and operations.

The Superior Hiking Trail has always been an ambitious undertaking, given the rugged landscapes of northern Minnesota, the unique patchwork of public and private lands the Trail crosses, and the Association's evolution over time to keep up with demands on the Trail.

Climate change and its repercussions present new challenges on the Trail, as warmer, wetter winters and increasingly extreme weather events threaten the resilience of the Trail and its infrastructure. The Association is committed to adapting and responding to protect the Trail and provide enduring access to it.

The value that the Superior Hiking Trail provides to everyone who sets foot upon it, as well as the communities along its route, is truly immeasurable—and worthy of the investment. It will take steadfast support and stewardship from Trail users to keep the SHT one of the premier natural surface footpaths in the country. ⋀⋀

How to Use the Superior Hiking Trail

ACCESS THE TRAIL

Find a Trailhead. Over 60 trailhead parking areas provide access to the Superior Hiking Trail. All SHT trailheads feature a trailhead sign, and in some locations, signs along major roadways indicate where to turn to reach the trailhead. Trailhead locations can be found on Area Locator maps in each chapter, and driving directions and GPS waypoints for each trailhead can be found under *Beginning Trailhead* for each section of the SHT. Trailheads are also indicated on all maps published by the Superior Hiking Trail Association. For the most current driving directions to SHT trailheads, the Association recommends entering the GPS waypoints provided into a navigation tool (such as Google Maps) before departing, as many trailheads do not have street addresses and are located outside of cell coverage.

What to Expect at SHT Trailheads. Each SHT trailhead provides, at a minimum, space for a few cars to park. Some trailheads are located within state parks or at other recreation sites or waysides, which may offer access to toilets, water, and other facilities. Most SHT trailheads do not have toilets or trash cans available, so plan accordingly. Size and capacity vary considerably between trailheads. For example, the Bally Creek Road Trailhead has capacity for only a few cars, while the Jay Cooke State Park Visitor Center has room for many. Some trailheads are shared with other trail systems and their users, which means they may experience more use at different times of the year. Trailhead capacity and facilities are listed under Beginning Trailhead for each section of the Trail.

Many trailheads are located on a spur trail that connects the trailhead to the main SHT. Spur trail mileage is indicated in italics in the Mileage Chart for each section of the Trail.

Trailhead Etiquette. Much like the Superior Hiking Trail itself, trailheads are to be shared and used responsibly. Park efficiently to save space for other users, and carpool to the trailhead whenever possible to reduce congestion. If a trailhead is full upon arrival, please find another trailhead to avoid crowding. Do not camp, sleep in a car overnight, stash supplies, or leave behind garbage at any trailhead.

Most SHT trailheads allow overnight parking, but some have restrictions on how long parking is allowed or permit requirements. No permit, reservation, or fee is required for most SHT trailheads. However, trailheads within state parks typically require a day-use or annual permit, and overnight parking typically requires checking in with park staff. These restrictions and requirements are listed under Beginning Trailhead for each section of the SHT. Always follow posted signage for the most current parking rules at SHT trailheads.

When a "Trail" Isn't a Trail. First-time visitors to the Superior Hiking Trail and northern Minnesota broadly may notice a charming, but potentially confusing instance of roads with "Trail" in their name. There are several examples along the SHT:

• Sawbill Trail near Tofte, Minnesota is a major road leading into the Superior National Forest.

• Caribou Trail near Lutsen, Minnesota is not a footpath, but a wide, paved road.

• Gunflint Trail near Grand Marais, Minnesota is a major road passageway to the Boundary Waters Canoe Area.

• Arrowhead Trail is a dirt road that provides access to some of the northernmost SHT trailheads.

Keep this in mind to avoid confusion when navigating to and along the Superior Hiking Trail.

USE THE TRAIL

The Superior Hiking Trail is managed with the following activities in mind:

Day Hiking: Convenient trailheads make it possible to explore the Superior Hiking Trail in day-sized hikes of any length. Shuttle providers service most of the Superior Hiking Trail, but often day hikers enjoy the experience of hiking from the trailhead and turning around to return to where they parked. The view is always different coming back! Many users have completed the entire SHT through day hikes of each section of the Trail.

Loops are another excellent way to explore the Superior Hiking Trail by day hiking. While the SHTA maintains several loops, users should also consider state park trails and other nearby public trail systems that connect to the SHT. With these trail networks, loops can be created by using a map and some creativity. Some popular loops, like the Bean and Bear Lakes Loop, are typically very busy during peak times; solitude may be better found on lesser-known loops.

Trail Running: The Superior Hiking Trail is known for its challenging, technical terrain for trail running. Besides rocks and roots, the Trail provides hefty accumulative elevation gains for lung- and leg-burning workouts. The Trail is host to several trail races each year.

Backpacking: The Superior Hiking Trail Association maintains 94 campsites for backpackers. Campsites include a fire ring, backcountry latrine, tent pads, and most have suitable trees for hammocking. Not every campsite has a reliable water source, so plan accordingly and always filter or treat your water. Most Superior Hiking Trail campsites are located on a short spur trail off of the main SHT. The few campsites located at the end of longer spur trails have the distance of the spur noted in the description of the campsite.

Campsites are available year-round and must be shared with other parties—they cannot be reserved or claimed for exclusive use. Campsites are free, but require users to abide by rules posted at each SHT campsite; this is explained in detail on page 14. Due to the proliferation of private lands on and near the Trail, backpackers must stay in these designated sites or nearby fee campgrounds to protect the Trail.

Adjacent state park camping, both at campgrounds and at hike-in sites near the Superior Hiking Trail, must be reserved ahead of time and require payment through the state park reservation system.

Long-distance hiking and thru-hiking (hiking the length of the entire Trail in one long trip) require significant planning prior to the trip. Resupplying one's food can be a challenge in the remote areas the SHT traverses. Visit the Association's website for more information on resupply planning.

Winter Use: Many sections of the SHT are ideal for winter use. Snowshoes and other winter-appropriate footwear can facilitate wondrous winter adventures. Be sure to stay off any groomed ski trails and avoid post-holing when snow is soft. Beware of ice and consider using gear that provides better traction on icy surfaces when appropriate. Not all trailheads are maintained for winter use, so check the Trailhead Index (page 204) before heading out and always have a backup plan.

NAVIGATE THE TRAIL

The Superior Hiking Trail is primarily marked by trail signs and blazes. Blazes are painted rectangles typically found on trees and rocks near eye level at helpful intervals to reassure users they're still on the Trail. Some turns in the Trail are marked with two blazes, one slightly higher than the other. The higher blaze indicates the direction the Trail turns.

Follow blue blazes for the main SHT and white blazes for spur trails to places like overlooks, campsites, or trailheads off the main SHT. Every SHT campsite is marked with a sign along the main trail corridor. Some areas of the SHT feature map signs to assist in navigation. Always use caution at intersections with roads and other trails. Always carry a paper map and a compass— and know how to use them.

The Superior Hiking Trail Association publishes and regularly updates other resources to help plan trips and navigate the Trail. In addition to this guidebook, the SHTA has published the *Superior Hiking Trail Databook,* a compact guide, and the *Trail Atlas of the Superior Hiking Trail,* a comprehensive set of trail maps available in print and digital formats. Check the website for more information and updates.

SHUTTLES AND OTHER SERVICES

The Superior Hiking Trail Association does not operate a shuttle service for trail users, but several private businesses offer scheduled and customized shuttle services to SHT trailheads. Shuttles are a great option for long-distance hikers or trail users who prefer to travel one direction without leaving a car at either end of the trip. Visit superiorhiking.org/shuttles for more details on shuttle services near the Trail.

Many lodges, hotels, campgrounds, and outfitters operate along or near the Superior Hiking Trail, and local tourism and visitor information centers are available to assist with planning a visit to the area. Find current links to these resources at superiorhiking.org/services.

SEASONAL CONSIDERATIONS

Spring: Snow does not typically melt until mid- to late-May. Spring thaw mud can be a challenge to walk or run through, and in some cases, footprints may leave a lasting mark on the Trail. Ticks, mosquitos, and black flies emerge at the end of May or sooner, especially if there is warmer weather. Weather and trail conditions vary greatly between the northern and southern ends of the Trail. Consider planning a major trip for another time of year, and be sure to stay off the Trail when it is saturated with water to avoid causing damage. See page 15 for seasonal closures of the SHT in Duluth.

Summer: Ticks, mosquitoes, and black flies will be present. In dry years, smaller water sources may be unreliable by late summer. In very dry years, a campfire ban may also be in effect. Expect to share the Trail, trailheads, and campsites with other users.

Fall: Typically, bugs are gone after the first frost. The fall color (or leaf peeping) season is one of the busiest times on the SHT, so have a backup plan if your preferred trailhead is full. See page 15 for hunting closures and seasonal closures of the SHT in Duluth.

Winter: Winter conditions in northern Minnesota can be extreme and dangerous, so be sure to plan and dress accordingly. The challenge of winter hiking, running, or snowshoeing is rewarded by stunning winter silence, solitude, and winter-only scenery. Backpacking and camping at SHT campsites in winter is recommended for experienced users only.

At any time of the year, northern Minnesota weather conditions can vary greatly on the Superior Hiking Trail. Extreme weather events can impact the experience on the Trail and create dangerous conditions, make the Trail difficult to navigate, or even require closures of the Trail. Check weather forecasts in advance and always check Trail Conditions on the Association's website. ⋀⋀

Protect the Trail and Yourself

As a user of the Superior Hiking Trail, you play a vital role in ensuring it remains safe, accessible, and enjoyable for thousands of other users. It is imperative to minimize impacts and protect this resource and the natural environment surrounding it.

If you or another Trail user needs medical attention or a law-enforcement response, call 911 immediately. Search and Rescue services in each county may be contacted directly or through 911.

If you see something, say something; to report damage, bad behavior, an aggressive animal, or other issues on the Trail, please visit superiorhiking.org to submit an incident report.

PLEASE OBSERVE THE FOLLOWING WHILE ENJOYING THE SUPERIOR HIKING TRAIL:

Respect the environment. If you pack it in, you should pack it out. Keep an eye out for micro-trash. Do not collect any natural or cultural objects. When nature calls, use a latrine. If a latrine is not available, please dig a small hole 6-8 inches deep, 4-6 inches in diameter, and at least 200 feet from a water source. Fill it in and camouflage when finished. Never use soap in a lake or stream. Carry water 200 feet away from water sources to clean dishes or yourself. Walk single-file to avoid widening the Trail and trampling nearby plants. Walk through mud puddles to avoid further damage to the area, and stay off the Trail if the tread is soggy and saturated with water. Observe wildlife from a safe distance and don't disturb the animals. Remember you are a visitor in their home.

Respect fellow trail users. Protect the quality of the Superior Hiking Trail experience for other users by avoiding loud voices and noises and being courteous when sharing campsites or meeting others on the Trail.

Respect private landowner rights by staying on the Trail. Private lands on the SHT are often unmarked. The Association's agreements with landowners have promised that SHT users will remain on the Trail at all times. When accessing the SHT, please only use SHT designated trailheads and/or walk-in access from other public trail systems, such as state park trails. Stay away from informal road crossings; these are not designated for a reason.

Dogs are allowed on the Trail, but must be kept on-leash at all times. You must be responsible for your dog—keep them under control at all times and pack out all pet waste.

The SHT is for foot travel only, except where the Trail shares a section with another multi-use trail. If you encounter a horse on a shared trail, yield to the horse and communicate with the rider before passing to ensure safety. If you encounter a bike on a shared trail, bikers should yield to foot traffic.

Do not cache food or supplies on the Trail, at campsites, or at trailheads.

Let someone know your plans in advance. The SHT is not patrolled. Take responsibility for sharing plans and checking in for safety. Cell phone coverage is inconsistent along the Trail. A call to 911 or a text message may get through even when service may not allow a normal voice call.

Practice basic safety and self-care on the Trail. Perform a thorough tick check after using the Trail to avoid tick-borne illness. Treat or filter water from sources along the Trail. Carry food, water, first aid supplies, and other essential items.

PLEASE OBSERVE THE FOLLOWING WHEN ENJOYING SUPERIOR HIKING TRAIL CAMPSITES:

Camp only at designated Superior Hiking Trail campsites. Camping is not allowed at SHT trailheads. Many trailheads are on or near private lands. Only camp at state park fee sites after reserving and paying for the site.

Campsites and campsite infrastructure must be shared by parties. SHT campsites are "all come, all served." Please make space to welcome fellow campers.

Break up large groups to avoid overcrowding. Most SHT campsites are designed to be enjoyed by 9 or fewer people at a time. Refer to campsite descriptions for the capacity and availability of each campsite.

Observe any fire restrictions while on the Trail, and do not create new fire rings.

Always hang food with a bear bag or use a bear canister.

Leave the campsite better than you found it.

If a latrine is full, do not use it. Dig a cat hole 200 feet outside camp and 200 feet away from all water access. Please report full latrines to the Superior Hiking Trail Association. Do not throw anything except for toilet paper into latrines.

SEASONAL CLOSURES

While much of the Superior Hiking Trail is hosted on public lands that remain open year-round, some sections of the Trail are closed periodically for trail user safety, to protect the Trail from damage, and to honor the wishes of public and private landowners.

Hunting Closures. To ensure your safety and to respect the many private landowners who allow access to their land, please check hunting season closure information posted at superiorhiking.org, respect any posted closures, and plan to only use the Trail within the City of Duluth boundaries during firearms deer season. Several other hunting seasons begin near the Trail each year on September 1, so wear blaze orange when using the Trail in the fall for additional safety. Visit the Minnesota Department of Natural Resources website for more information on hunting seasons.

Duluth Superior Hiking Trail Closures. The Superior Hiking Trail inside the City of Duluth (131st Ave W. Trailhead to Martin Road Trailhead) is typically closed each year during the spring thaw (approximately April through mid-May), and again in the fall before the ground freezes (approximately mid-October to mid-November). These closures are done in partnership with the Duluth Parks and Recreation to help protect the Trail when it is saturated with water and most susceptible to damage. Plan accordingly and respect our partnership with the City. ⋀⋀

The Lands of the
Superior Hiking Trail

The Superior Hiking Trail is located on the traditional, ancestral, and contemporary lands of the Anishinaabeg people. The Trail is intrinsically tied to the many lands it crosses, which include a complicated patchwork of public and private ownership. Today, the Superior Hiking Trail Association coordinates permissions from over 200 landowners and land managers, totaling nearly 1,500 parcels of land.

The Superior Hiking Trail passes through eight state parks, all administered by the Minnesota Department of Natural Resources (DNR). But the Trail is also hosted on several other types of DNR-administered land such as state forests and school trust lands. All together, more than 150 miles of the Superior Hiking Trail are on DNR-administered lands.

Nearly 70 miles of the Superior Hiking Trail fall within the Superior National Forest, administered by the United States Forest Service. Several pieces of the Superior Hiking Trail were constructed in the Superior National Forest before the concept of the SHT even existed.

The Superior Hiking Trail passes through four counties and onto lands owned by each of the four: Carlton, St. Louis, Lake, and Cook counties all oversee lands which host the SHT, for a total of over 35 miles.

The City of Duluth is a major landowner and partner, with over 40 miles of the Superior Hiking Trail falling within city limits.

Finally but crucially, nearly 45 miles of the Superior Hiking Trail is on private property. Private lands exist on most sections of the Superior Hiking Trail, often forming a crucial link between public lands. While this private land is concentrated in the vicinity of Two Harbors, it also makes up large portions of the Trail near Silver Bay and Finland, where private entities such as North Shore Mining and Wolf Ridge Environmental Learning Center graciously host the Trail on their large properties. Agreements between the Association and private landowners vary from permanent easements to limited access arrangements.

Partnerships with landowners and managers take many forms. The Association relies on support from our partners to maintain shared trail infrastructure, collaborate on trail improvement projects, secure funding, and much more. It is critical for all Trail users to respect public and private land. Stay on the Trail, and practice Leave No Trace to ensure access now and for decades to come. ⋀⋀

Other Trails of the North Shore

While the Superior Hiking Trail is the premier foot-travel trail on the North Shore of Lake Superior, it intersects many other long-distance trails. These other trails may be used in conjunction with the Superior Hiking Trail to create loops, or they can be enjoyed by themselves.

North Country National Scenic Trail. The North Country National Scenic Trail (NCT) is a nearly 5,000-mile trail that spans from North Dakota to Vermont. The Superior Hiking Trail is a part of the NCT's route through Minnesota. The NCT extends into Wisconsin from the Superior Hiking Trail's southern terminus. The NCT in Wisconsin is managed by the North Country Trail Association, and maps can be found on their website.

Willard Munger State Trail. Intersecting several times in the Jay Cooke State Park and Duluth sections of the Superior Hiking Trail, the Willard Munger State Trail is a paved, multi-use trail. Besides creating loop options, it also enables trail users to bike-shuttle themselves between trailheads. Administered by the Minnesota Department of Natural Resources, maps can be found on their website.

DWP Trail. The DWP Trail is a 10-mile trail along the abandoned route of the former Duluth, Winnipeg and Pacific (DWP) railroad. It is known for its two steel trestles and a tunnel under Ely's Peak. The wide, gentle grade of the trail makes it suitable for multiple uses including mobility-limited users, biking, hiking or running, cross-country skiing, equestrians, and snowshoeing. The DWP acts as a spine for all trail networks in West Duluth.

Duluth Traverse. The Duluth Traverse is a multi-use trail optimized for mountain bikes. It connects well-known greenspaces in Duluth such as the Mission Creek area near Fond du Lac, Spirit Mountain Recreation Area, Brewer Park, and Hartley Park, intersecting many times with the Superior Hiking Trail. The Duluth Traverse Trail network is estimated to someday reach over 100 miles. Maps and more information can be found on the Duluth Parks and Recreation website.

Cross City Trail/Duluth Lakewalk. The SHT shares portions of urban paved trail systems within the City of Duluth. These trails connect SHT users to amenities and points of interest in the Duluth area.

North Shore State Trail. The North Shore State Trail (NSST) is a 146-mile multi-use trail from Martin Road Trailhead in Duluth to Grand Marais. In key locations, it briefly shares its route with the Superior Hiking Trail and intersects the SHT many times. Additionally, several trailheads are shared by users of the SHT and NSST, which means these trailheads are often plowed in the winter. The North Shore State Trail is primarily used as a snowmobile trail, but other uses are allowed, including horseback riding, biking, and hiking. One section near Finland is also open to all-terrain vehicles. This trail often runs through soggy areas and due to its emphasis on winter use, very few if any structures, other than large bridges, exist along its path. Still, the NSST has many stretches that are enjoyable for foot travel. The trail may have high grass and minimal signage leading to a wide yet still wild trail. The NSST intersects with many other snowmobile trails, at times creating confusing intersections. Administered by the Minnesota Department of Natural Resources, maps can be found on their website.

Gitchi-Gami State Trail. The paved Gitchi-Gami State Trail parallels Highway 61 between Two Harbors and Grand Marais. Over 30 miles are completed out of an estimated 90 miles with more progress taking place each year. Besides creating loop options (particularly in the Split Rock Lighthouse State Park and Tofte areas), it also enables trail users to bike-shuttle themselves between trailheads. This trail is administered by the Gitchi-Gami Trail Association.

Border Route Trail (North Country Trail). For trail users wanting to continue past the Superior Hiking Trail's northern terminus, the Border Route Trail heads west through the Boundary Waters Canoe Area for 65 miles and connects to the Kekekabic Trail. Both these trails host the route of the North Country Trail. Maps and more information can be found on the Border Route Trail Association website. ⋏⋏

How to Use the Guidebook

WHAT IS INCLUDED IN THIS GUIDEBOOK

There are thousands of possible details to describe the Superior Hiking Trail, and this guidebook does not include them all. Great care has been taken by the SHTA to present the most important information to help plan an enjoyable trip and navigate the Trail.

While the *Guidebook* is written primarily for the northbound trail user, it is also compatible with southbound trail usage. Mileage information is provided for both directions in the mileage chart for each section. Please note: The SHT travels predominantly southwest to northeast. There are several instances where a cardinal direction is used to be concise, but the true direction is southwest or northeast. *(Example: Ely's Peak Loop Spur **north** junction, which is slightly northeast of the south junction.)* If you have questions about true cardinal directions, please consult maps of the Superior Hiking Trail.

SEGMENTS AND SECTIONS

In the trail information resources published by the Association, the SHT has been split up into six segments of approximately 50 miles. Each segment of the Trail features many shorter trail sections from one trailhead to the next:

- Southern Terminus to Martin Road Trailhead
- Martin Road Trailhead to Lake County Road 301 Trailhead
- Lake County Road 301 Trailhead to Minnesota Highway 1 Trailhead
- Minnesota Highway 1 Trailhead to Temperance River State Wayside Trailhead
- Temperance River State Wayside Trailhead to Pincushion Mountain Trailhead
- Pincushion Mountain Trailhead to Northern Terminus

Guidebook chapters have been written to align with these segments, which are also used in the *Superior Hiking Trail Databook* and the *Trail Atlas for the Superior Hiking Trail,* to more easily coordinate between these resources. Each chapter contains an overview of the segment and more detailed information for each section, trailhead, campsite, and spur trail. See the example below for descriptions of what each field indicates:

▌ Beginning Trailhead to Ending Trailhead

(Example: Lax Lake Road Trailhead to Penn Boulevard Trailhead)

BEGINNING TRAILHEAD

Directions and GPS Waypoints: *Driving directions to the trailhead and waypoints to find the trailhead online or in navigation tool.*

Facilities: *Any features such as toilets, water, or other amenities.*

Size: *Approximate capacity of the trailhead, listed as:*

- *Small (5 or fewer vehicles)*
- *Medium (up to 20 vehicles)*
- *Large (20+ vehicles)*

Overnight parking: *If overnight parking is allowed or not allowed.*

Winter access: *If a trailhead is typically plowed during the winter.*

Special notes: *Anything else important to note about the trailhead.*

Trail Atlas map: *The corresponding map from the* Trail Atlas for the Superior Hiking Trail *or* Map Series Set. *(Example: C-5, C-6, the two maps that detail the Lax Lake Road to Penn Boulevard section)*

Total distance: *Main trail mileage for the SHT. When applicable, spur trail mileage to access the main SHT is listed in parentheses.*

Elevation change: *General amount of elevation change to expect on this section.*

SHT campsites: *Number of SHT campsites in this section.*

Hazards and concerns: *Anything noteworthy beyond the typical rugged (rooty, rocky, and uneven) features of the Trail.*

Synopsis: *This briefly describes the section's highlights and what to expect.*

CAMPSITE

▲ **Name of campsite** *(Example: Southwest Split Rock River Campsite)*

Size: *Approximate number of tent pads listed as:*

- *Small (2-3 tent pads)*
- *Medium (4-5 tent pads)*
- *Large (6 or more tent pads)*

Note: what constitutes a tent pad is extremely subjective; the estimates included in this book are meant as a general guide.

Water source: *Name or description of nearby water. Known fluctuations in water availability will be noted here. If there is not a source of water in the immediate vicinity of a campsite, the nearest reliable source is listed.*

Description of campsite *(Example: Campsite is often heavily used during peak periods.)*

Distance to next campsites *(Example: 6.7, 2.7 ⊖ ⊕ 7.3, 13.4)*

Mileage to neighboring campsites is located underneath each campsite in the text. Each campsite listing includes the cumulative mileage to the next two campsites in each direction. Campsites located to the southwest are on the left, and campsites located to the northeast are to the right. If you're traveling southbound, your next two campsites are 2.7 and 6.7 miles away. If you're heading northbound, you'll have to travel 7.3 and 13.4 miles to reach the next two campsites.

■ **Name of spur trail** *(Example: Cascade River Loop Spur)*
Brief description of the spur trail with any important details to note (Example: A 3.5-mile spur trail makes up the eastern half of the Cascade River Loop. The crossing of Trout Creek is unbridged, but generally easy to cross except after a large rain event or during snowmelt.)

Mileage Chart. Rules for italicization in Mileage: *Spur trails are italicized. Trailheads located on spur trails are italicized.*

MAPS

Map Legend

Superior Hiking Trail	——
Spur Trails	············
Other Trails	--------
Trailhead	**P**
SHT backcountry campsite	**Λ**
State Park or commercial campsite	**$Λ**
Primary road	—(35)(61)—
County or Secondary road	—(70)—
Forest or township road	—[336]—

Segment Overview Maps. An overview map of each segment of the Trail is provided to assist with navigation to trailheads.

Section Highlight Maps. Several detailed maps of unique and interesting sections of Trail are provided to help explore the SHT in these areas.

Additional Maps Available. The Superior Hiking Trail Association has published additional maps for the Trail: the *Trail Atlas for the Superior Hiking Trail* and *Map Series Sets.* Both are available in print and digital formats. Paper versions of these maps can be purchased on the Association's website or from a local outdoor retailer; digital versions can be purchased through the Avenza Maps mobile app.

CAMPSITE DISTANCE INDEX

For long-distance planning convenience, an index of distances between all campsites is listed on page 200. Campsites are listed from South to North, with mileage provided for northbound and southbound travel and approximate campsite size.

TRAILHEAD INDEX

To quickly find out if a trailhead offers overnight parking or winter access, refer to the Trailhead Index on page 204.

Please note: Several trailhead names have been changed from previous SHTA publications to reflect the most up-to-date, accurate information and to help trail users more easily navigate to these trailheads. In many cases, trailhead names have been updated from a road number to the common, signed name of the road *(Example: Cook County Road 58 Trailhead is now referred to as Lindskog Road Trailhead.)*

If you are uncertain about which trailheads these new names reference, you can find more information online at superiorhiking.org/trailheadupdates. ⋀⋀

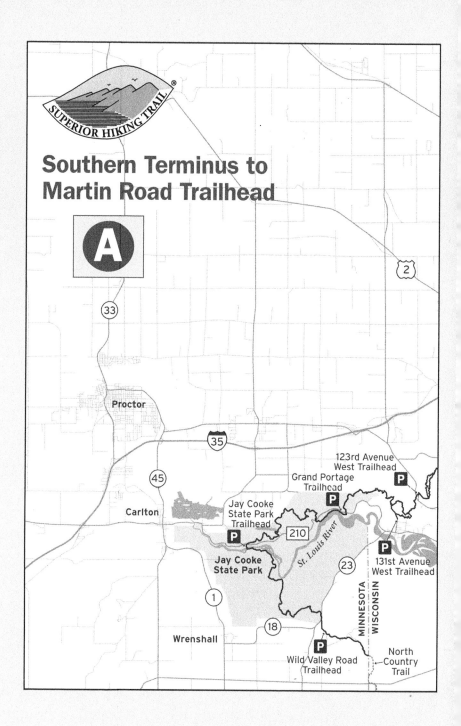

Southern Terminus to Martin Road Trailhead

A

33

Proctor

35

123rd Avenue West Trailhead **P**

45

Grand Portage Trailhead **P**

Carlton

Jay Cooke State Park Trailhead **P**

210

Jay Cooke State Park

St. Louis River

23

131st Avenue West Trailhead **P**

1

MINNESOTA

WISCONSIN

18

Wrenshall

P Wild Valley Road Trailhead

North Country Trail

2

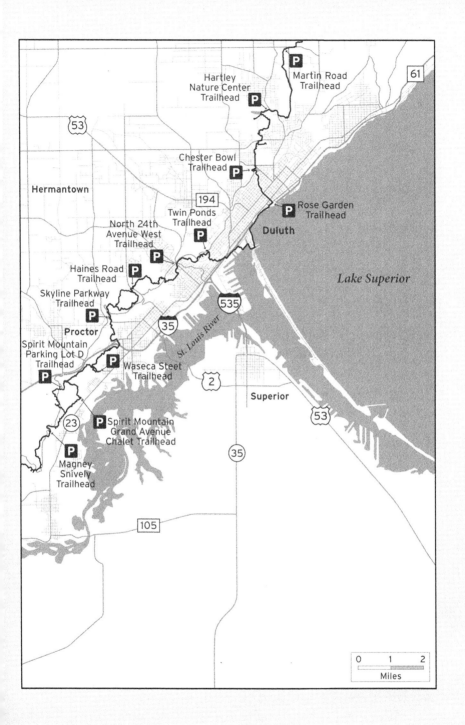

Hartley
Nature Center
Trailhead

Martin Road
Trailhead

61

53

Chester Bowl
Trailhead

Hermantown

194

Twin Ponds
Trailhead

Rose Garden
Trailhead

North 24th
Avenue West
Trailhead

Duluth

Haines Road
Trailhead

Lake Superior

Skyline Parkway
Trailhead

535

Proctor

35

St. Louis River

Spirit Mountain
Parking Lot D
Trailhead

Waseca Steet
Trailhead

2

Superior

23

Spirit Mountain
Grand Avenue
Chalet Trailhead

53

35

Magney
Snively
Trailhead

105

0	1	2

Miles

27

Southern Terminus to Martin Road Trailhead

▌ Overview

The southern terminus of the Superior Hiking Trail is located at the Minnesota-Wisconsin state line where a quaint wooden archway denotes the terminus and welcomes visitors to the North Country National Scenic Trail in Wisconsin. To reach the terminus, one must travel out and back from Wild Valley Road Trailhead, or find a parking area in Wisconsin to travel one way—there is no road access at the southern terminus.

Heading north from the terminus, the Superior Hiking Trail crosses a fiberglass bridge spanning the tiny Red River: a significant crossing that was considered the "missing link" that made the entire SHT contiguous from top to bottom when the bridge was built in 2017.

Wild Valley Road Trailhead is the southernmost trailhead of the Superior Hiking Trail. After a short walk down Wild Valley Road and along Minnesota Highway 23, the Trail enters Jay Cooke State Park. Along this stretch, the Trail passes a view of a railroad trestle and the valley carved out by the St. Louis River. Inside the park, the Trail follows foot travel-only pathways and multi-use trails groomed for skiing before crossing the St. Louis River on the historic Swinging Bridge, rebuilt after the 2012 flood.

Shortly beyond the bridge is **Jay Cooke State Park Visitor Center Trailhead.** From here the Superior Hiking Trail continues to alternate between natural footpath and multi-use trails, including a short bit on the paved Willard Munger State Trail. Watch carefully for blue blazes and Superior Hiking Trail signs to stay on the route. After crossing

Minnesota Highway 210 (the first of two crossings), the Trail follows the St. Louis River along the historic and serene Grand Portage Trail.

At **Grand Portage Trailhead,** another trailhead within the boundaries of Jay Cooke State Park, the Superior Hiking Trail travels on state park trails to another crossing of Highway 210. The Trail climbs a narrow ridge to the park boundary and comes to a historic stone bridge over Mission Creek. Throughout this area, the Trail travels up and down ridges with steep ravines on either side, shaded occasionally by massive white pines. A spur trail descends from the ridges down to the bank of Mission Creek and a trailhead.

The **131st Avenue West Trailhead** features two spur trails connecting to the main Superior Hiking Trail. The western spur trail is preferred and foot travel-only, following the lovely Mission Creek. The other multi-use spur trail can be used to make a loop back to the trailhead or to access the middle of this section. Beyond this spur trail junction, the Superior Hiking Trail descends to cross Sargent Creek and ascends to Becks Road.

The **123rd Avenue West Trailhead** connects the Superior Hiking Trail with the paved Willard Munger State Trail for a brief overlap before encountering Ely's Peak Loop and a steep climb on rugged trail and rock faces up to Ely's Peak. The expansive views showcase the St. Louis River Estuary, one of the largest freshwater estuaries in the country. Many short spurs lead to overlooks as the Trail enters the old growth forests of the Magney-Snively Natural Area.

A short spur trail connects the **Magney-Snively Trailhead** to the main Superior Hiking Trail, which soon follows Skyline Parkway over a historic stone bridge before descending into the woods. The Trail skirts ruins and a unique stone canal along Gogebic Creek before entering Spirit Mountain Recreation Area, where the Spirit Mountain Loop Spur connects to fee-based Spirit Mountain Recreation Area Campground. The main Superior Hiking Trail travels around and through Spirit Mountain, crossing the bottom of a ski slope near the Grand Avenue Chalet. Expect to find snow on the hills well into the spring.

From the **Grand Avenue Chalet Trailhead,** the Superior Hiking Trail ascends along the edge of a ski run and follows Knowlton Creek steadily uphill before crossing the creek and ascending to a woods on the edge of railroad tracks. When the Trail arrives at Kingsbury Creek, it follows the cascading creek to a spur trail leading to Waseca Street.

The **Waseca Street Trailhead,** near the Lake Superior Zoo, connects to the main Superior Hiking Trail via a short spur trail. The Trail follows Kingsbury Creek uphill, turning away from the creek and leading to a series of small rocky outcroppings that offer sweeping views. The Superior Hiking Trail descends to the Cross City Trail, following it for a short distance underneath I-35 before turning uphill, navigating the edge of several neighborhoods, and eventually arriving at Keene Creek.

From the **Skyline Parkway Trailhead,** the Superior Hiking Trail continues to follow Keene Creek, a sweet prelude to the stretch of the Trail that contains the Brewer Park Loop. The Superior Hiking Trail follows the ridgeline and offers dramatic views of downtown Duluth, Park Point, Lake Superior, and the City of Superior in Wisconsin. The Trail makes a sharp descent off the Brewer Park ridge and goes through a tunnel under Haines Road.

The **Haines Road Trailhead** connects to the main Superior Hiking Trail by a short spur trail on a sidewalk. The Trail climbs to several open vistas of Lake Superior and the St. Louis River Estuary before descending to pass through the Lincoln Park neighborhood. After crossing Miller Creek, the Superior Hiking Trail comes out of the woods and arrives at a trailhead.

At the **North 24th Avenue West Trailhead,** the Superior Hiking Trail follows a short stretch of sidewalk along Skyline Parkway. The SHT returns to the woods on its way to Enger Tower, a historic landmark; if you choose to add some vertical climb, the five-story climb will provide 360-degree views of Duluth. The Twin Ponds Trailhead is just a short climb down from the tower, and the Trail continues downhill to eventually cross a pedestrian bridge over I-35. The Trail is paved from this point until Chester Park as it passes local attractions: Bayfront

Festival Park; the William S. Irvin, a restored Great Lakes ship; and the iconic Aerial Lift Bridge. The Superior Hiking Trail shares Duluth's famous Lakewalk to leave Canal Park Business District.

At Leif Erickson Park and the **Rose Garden Trailhead,** the Superior Hiking Trail follows 14th Avenue East before entering Chester Park. The Trail follows the Chester Creek gorge. After passing under Skyline Parkway, the Trail turns to climb away from the creek up a steep hill toward the University of Minnesota-Duluth campus. The Superior Hiking Trail enters Bagley Nature Area, which features a Lake Superior vista and a fee campground managed by the University. The Trail enters Hartley Park, passes Hartley Pond, and arrives at the next trailhead at Hartley Nature Center.

The Superior Hiking Trail departs **Hartley Nature Center Trailhead,** soon coming to a 1.6-mile roadwalk through quaint neighborhoods and among cemeteries. The Superior Hiking Trail leaves the gravel Vermilion Road to head back into the woods where it passes through Downer Park. The route offers peeks into a small, steep gorge of Amity Creek. The journey through the City of Duluth officially comes to an end at Martin Road Trailhead. ⋏⋏

▌ Southern Terminus to Wild Valley Road Trailhead

Directions and GPS Waypoints: Take I-35 Exit #235, go east on MN-210 for 2.4 miles to Carlton. Turn south on Carlton Co. Rd. 1, go 4.5 miles to Wrenshall, turn east on Carlton Co. Rd. 18, go 3.1 miles, turn north on MN-23, go 0.3 miles. Turn south on Wild Valley Rd., go 0.5 miles to parking lot on left. GPS: 46.618254, -92.320542

Facilities: None

Size: Small

Overnight parking: Allowed

Winter access: No

Special notes: Wild Valley Road is closed during the spring freeze-thaw cycle, usually until early May.

SECTION SNAPSHOT

Trail Atlas map: A-1

Total distance: 1.9 miles (3.8 miles if traveling out-and-back from Wild Valley Road Trailhead)

Elevation change: While there are some hills, this is a relatively gentle section.

SHT campsites: One

Hazards and concerns: The Trail in this area is adjacent to an area popular for target shooting. It is common to hear gunfire.

Synopsis: The Southern Terminus of the Superior Hiking Trail at the Minnesota-Wisconsin border is marked by a beautiful wooden arch and a trail register. There is no trailhead at the terminus, so users must travel out-and-back from Wild Valley Road Trailhead or find another parking area along the North Country Trail in Wisconsin. This section crosses the Red River over a fiberglass bridge and features the Red River Valley Campsite, the only SHTA campsite south of Martin Road.

▲ **Red River Valley Campsite**

Size: Medium

Water source: Tributary of the Red River

Campsite is in a pleasant wooded location above the river. Trains often pass near the campsite. This is the only SHTA campsite until Bald Eagle Campsite, north of Duluth. There are many fee campgrounds, campsites, and low-cost motel options throughout the City of Duluth.

⊖ 53.1, 54.3

MILEAGE	Northbound	Southbound
Superior Hiking Trail southern terminus, register	**0.0**	**1.9**
Red River bridge	0.3	1.6
Red River Valley Campsite	0.4	1.5
Mountain Goat Road junction	1.1	0.8
Wild Valley Road Trailhead	**1.9**	**0.0**

Wild Valley Road Trailhead to Jay Cooke State Park Visitor Center Trailhead

Directions and GPS Waypoints: Take I-35 Exit #235, go east on MN-210 for 2.4 miles to Carlton. Turn south on Carlton Co. Rd. 1, go 4.5 miles to Wrenshall, turn east on Carlton Co. Rd. 18, go 3.1 miles, turn north on MN-23, go 0.3 miles. Turn south on Wild Valley Rd., go 0.5 miles to parking lot on left. GPS: 46.618254, -92.320542

Facilities: None

Size: Small

Overnight parking: Allowed

Winter access: No

Special notes: Wild Valley Road is closed during the spring, usually until early May.

SECTION SNAPSHOT

Trail Atlas map: A-1, A-2

Total distance: 5.9 miles

Elevation change: A few steep climbs

SHT campsites: None. However, the Trail comes close to a few Jay Cooke State Park backpack-in campsites which must be reserved and paid for ahead of time.

Hazards and concerns: Watch for signage at several trail junctions to stay on the Superior Hiking Trail. Be careful on several steep, uneven staircases. Groomed ski trails are closed to foot travel during the winter.

Synopsis: After a 0.5-mile roadwalk from Wild Valley Road Trailhead, the Superior Hiking Trail turns into Jay Cooke State Park and offers nice vistas of the St. Louis River valley, particularly during leaf-off season. After a few steep staircases through cedar forest, the Trail follows cross-country ski trails through the park toward the historic Swinging Bridge over the St. Louis River before arriving at the park's River Inn Visitor Center.

MILEAGE	Northbound	Southbound
Wild Valley Road Trailhead	**0.0**	**5.9**
Wild Valley Road roadwalk east end	0.0	5.9
Wild Valley Road roadwalk west end, Minnesota Highway 23 crossing and roadwalk	0.4	5.5
Minnesota Highway 23 roadwalk north end	0.5	5.4
Railroad Bridge Vista	2.2	3.7
Power line corridor, nearby state park campsites (reservation and payment required)	3.5	2.4
Silver Creek bridge	4.1	1.8
Swinging Bridge over St. Louis River	5.8	0.1
Jay Cooke State Park Visitor Center Trailhead	**5.9**	**0.0**

▌ Jay Cooke State Park Visitor Center Trailhead to Grand Portage Trailhead

Directions and GPS Waypoints: Take I-35 Exit #235, go east on MN-210 5.5 miles to Jay Cooke State Park Visitor Center on right. GPS: 46.654645, -92.371080

Facilities: Park office, toilets, picnic area, state park fee campsites

Size: Large

Overnight parking: Allowed with state park permit. Please check in with state park staff.

Winter access: Yes

Special notes: A state park day-use or annual permit is required to park here.

SECTION SNAPSHOT

Trail Atlas map: A-2

Total distance: 5.9 miles

Elevation change: A few steep sections

Hazards and concerns: Watch for signage at several trail junctions to stay on the Superior Hiking Trail. Groomed ski trails are closed to foot travel during the winter. Use caution when crossing Minnesota Highway 210.

Synopsis: In this section, the Superior Hiking Trail follows a mix of multi-use and foot-travel only paths. Highlights include a crossing over a hydroelectric dam at Forbay Lake and a serene trek on the historic Grand Portage Trail along the banks of the St. Louis River.

MILEAGE	Northbound	Southbound
Jay Cooke State Park Visitor Center Trailhead	**0.0**	**5.9**
Minnesota Highway 210 crossing	0.1	5.8
Day-use shelter with vista	0.6	5.3
View of spillway	0.9	5.0
Power line corridor	1.5	4.4
Dam crossing	1.8	4.1
Multiple junctions with Willard Munger State Trail	2.6	3.3
Minnesota Highway 210 crossing	5.0	0.9
Bench	5.3	0.6
Minnesota Highway 210 roadwalk	5.9	0.0
Grand Portage Trailhead	**5.9**	**0.0**

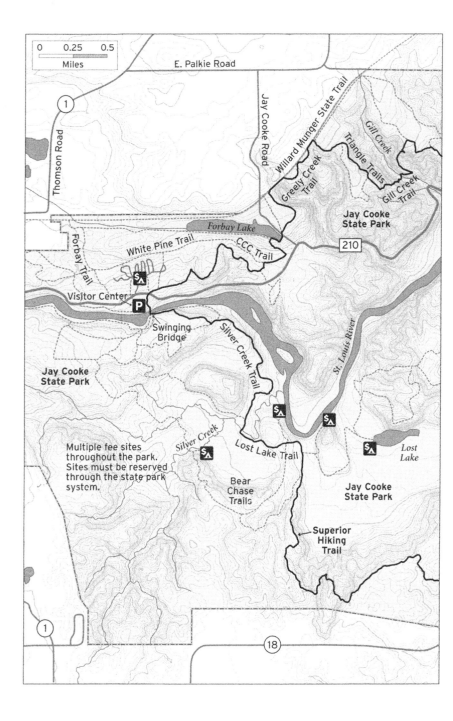

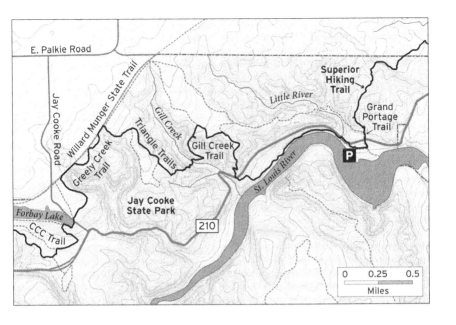

▍Grand Portage Trailhead to 131st Avenue West Trailhead

Directions and GPS Waypoints: Northbound: Take I-35 Exit #235, go east on MN-210 9.4 miles to Grand Portage parking lot on right. Southbound: From MN-23/MN-210 intersection, turn onto MN-210, go 2.4 miles to Grand Portage parking lot on left. GPS: 46.668182, -92.307914

Facilities: None

Size: Medium

Overnight parking: No

Winter access: Yes

Special notes: A state park day-use or annual permit is required to park here.

SECTION SNAPSHOT

Trail Atlas maps: A-2, A-3

Total distance: 3.5 miles (Additional 0.6-mile spur to 131st Avenue West Trailhead)

Elevation change: This section has a few steep climbs that can be particularly challenging in wet or icy conditions.

Hazards and concerns: Be careful on several steep, uneven staircases. Use caution when crossing Minnesota Highway 210.

Synopsis: The Superior Hiking Trail traverses rolling hills and creek valleys, often taking the high ground along ridgetops. Highlights are the historic Mission Creek stone bridge and the old pines that give this section a remote, northern feel.

MILEAGE	NORTHBOUND	SOUTHBOUND
Grand Portage Trailhead	**0.0**	**4.1**
Minnesota Highway 210 crossing	0.3	3.8
Grand Portage Trail junction	0.4	3.7
Power line corridor	1.0	3.1
Mission Creek stone bridge	2.3	1.8
Register, spur to 131st Avenue W. Trailhead	*3.5*	*0.6*
131st Avenue W. Trailhead	**4.1**	**0.0**

The Duluth SHT:
A Rugged, Urban Trail Experience

The Duluth segments of the Superior Hiking Trail were built in the 2000s, 20 years or more after the first 200 miles of the SHT to the north were constructed. Putting a natural surface footpath through an urban area had its unique challenges.

The Duluth SHT offers panoramic views of the waters below the hillsides of Duluth and frequently gives users a sense of remoteness. This section has many strengths—direct access to every neighborhood; proximity to amenities such as stores, restaurants, and multiple lodging options; and a glimpse into the historical and contemporary working industrial port. Its gritty, even quaint urban character sets it apart from the other 260 miles of the SHT.

Keep reading to learn more about the unique qualities of the Duluth SHT. ⋏⋏

▌ 131st Avenue West Trailhead to 123rd Avenue West Trailhead

Directions and GPS Waypoints: Northbound: Take I-35 Exit #246. Go south 4.5 miles on Becks Rd. to Commonwealth Ave./MN-23. Turn south, follow MN-23 3.8 miles, turn north on 131st Ave. W., go 0.4 miles to parking lot. Southbound: Take I-35 Exit #251B, go 8.7 miles, turn north on 131st Ave. W., go 0.4 miles to parking lot. GPS: 46.665863, -92.272477

Facilities: None

Size: Medium

Overnight parking: No

Winter access: No

Special notes: Follow white blazes and trail signage on a gravel road from the parking area to the junction of two possible spur trails—a 0.6-mile footpath or a 1.0-mile multi-use trail—that connect to the main Superior Hiking Trail.

SECTION SNAPSHOT

Trail Atlas map: A-3

Total distance: 1.8 miles (Additional 0.6-mile spur trail from 131st Avenue West Trailhead)

Elevation change: A few short elevation changes

Hazards and concerns: Use caution when crossing Beck's Road. If using the multi-use spur trail, be aware of mountain bike users sharing the trail.

Synopsis: Trail largely follows the top of a ridgeline to offer many viewpoints. Watch for the "Unimpressive Overlook" sign that leads to a surprisingly impressive panoramic view of the nearby valleys.

Pro tip: From the 131st Avenue West Trailhead, enjoy a nice 2.5-mile loop using the main SHT and the two spur trails that connect back to the trailhead.

MILEAGE	Northbound	Southbound
131st Avenue W. Trailhead	**0.0**	**2.4**
Register, spur from 131st Avenue W. Trailhead	*0.6*	*1.8*
Multi-use spur to 131st Avenue W. Trailhead	*1.5*	*0.9*
Sargent Creek bridge	1.9	0.5
Becks Road crossing	2.3	0.1
Spur to 123rd Avenue W. Trailhead	*2.4*	*0.0*
123rd Avenue W. Trailhead	**2.4**	**0.0**

The Duluth SHT:
A Rugged, Urban Trail Experience

Urban green space at its best. Duluth boasts one of the largest ratios of park land per capita in the country. When Duluth was developed, so was the vision for a world-class park system. The ethos of Fredrick Olmsted, America's most famous landscape architect, to preserve open spaces and separation from urban life, integrated into the Park system, preserving over 11,000 acres of green space within the City limits. In Duluth, the Trail passes through wooded creek ravines tucked into the urban landscape, rivaling for beauty and charm the northernmost sections of the SHT. What is probably more impressive is that locals have this landscape outside their backdoor. And while there may be no true wilderness in Duluth, it's easy to feel quite remote and removed. It is a city like no other, and the SHT traverses much of it! ⋀⋀

123rd Avenue West Trailhead to Magney-Snively Trailhead

Directions and GPS Waypoints: Northbound: Take I-35 Exit #246. Go south on Becks Rd. 2.7 miles. Turn north on 123rd Ave. W., go one block to parking lot. Southbound: Take I-35 Exit #251B, go south to Becks Rd. Turn west on Becks Rd., go 1.8 miles, turn north on 123rd Ave. W., go one block to parking lot. GPS: 46.676081, -92.258798

Facilities: None

Size: Large

Overnight parking: No

Winter access: Yes

Special notes: None

SECTION SNAPSHOT

Trail Atlas map: A-3

Total distance: 4.1 miles

Elevation change: A steep climb on rocky, uneven terrain up to Ely's Peak

Hazards and concerns: Steep, rocky, and uneven terrain. Watch for bikes on the paved Willard Munger State Trail.

Synopsis: Highlights include the challenging but rewarding Ely's Peak Loop, which features magnificent views and exposed rock faces, as well as a journey through the old-growth forests of the Magney-Snively Natural Area.

SPUR TRAILS

■ **Ely's Peak Loop.** A 1.3-mile spur trail connects to the main Superior Hiking Trail to create a 3-mile loop. The spur can also be enjoyed as a less rugged route up from the Willard Munger State Trail. It has sweeping vistas, including Larry's Lookout.

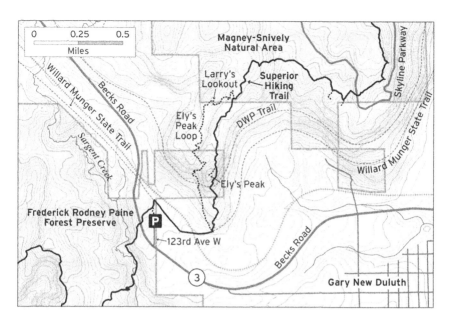

SPUR TRAILS, continued

▋ **Vista Overlooks.** There are many short, unnamed spur trails to scenic overlooks.

MILEAGE	Northbound	Southbound
123rd Avenue W. Trailhead	**0.0**	**4.1**
Spur from 133rd Avenue W. Trailhead	*0.0*	*4.1*
Willard Munger State Trail junction west end	0.1	4.0
Willard Munger State Trail junction east end	0.4	3.7
Ely's Peak Loop Spur south junction	0.4	3.7
Spur to Ely's Peak	0.9	3.2
Ely's Peak Loop Spur north junction	1.3	2.8
W. Skyline Parkway crossing	2.3	1.8
W. Skyline Parkway crossing	3.8	0.3
Spur to Magney Snively Trailhead	*4.1*	*0.0*
Magney Snively Trailhead	**4.1**	**0.0**

▌ Magney-Snively Trailhead to Spirit Mountain Grand Avenue Chalet Trailhead

Directions and GPS Waypoints: Take I-35 Exit #249. Go south on Boundary Ave. 0.2 miles, turn east on Skyline Parkway, go 1.5 miles to parking lot on left. GPS: 46.702179, -92.226880

Facilities: None

Size: Medium

Overnight parking: No

Winter access: Yes

Special notes: Trailhead is shared with horse riders and Nordic skiers.

SECTION SNAPSHOT

Trail Atlas maps: A-3, A-4

Total distance: 1.8 miles

Elevation change: A few short hills, but relatively gentle terrain

Hazards and concerns: Use caution on the Skyline Parkway roadwalk.

Synopsis: The Superior Hiking Trail leaves the woods to follow a short roadwalk on Skyline Parkway, which includes a stone bridge crossing over Stewart Creek. Watch for a spur trail to the Stewart Knob Overlook and a small bridge over Gogebic Creek. As the Trail enters Spirit Mountain Recreation Area, signs mark the junction with the Spirit Mountain Loop Spur.

SPUR TRAIL

■ **Spirit Mountain Loop.** A 1.9-mile loop spur can be combined with the main Superior Hiking Trail to create a 3.5-mile loop around the Spirit Mountain Recreation Area with several convenient access points. Spur trail also passes through the Spirit Mountain Campground, a fee camping area optimally located for backpackers travelling through Duluth.

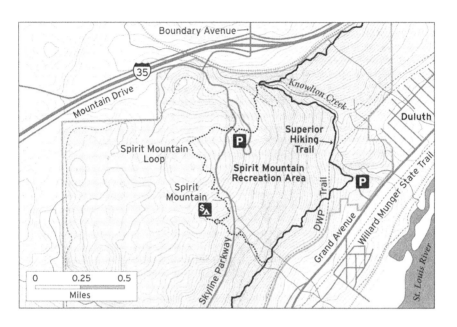

MILEAGE	Northbound	Southbound
Magney Snively Trailhead	**0.0**	**1.8**
Spur from Magney Snively Trailhead	0.0	1.8
W. Skyline Parkway roadwalk south end	0.1	1.7
Spur to Steward Knob Overlook	0.1	1.7
Stewart Creek stone bridge	0.2	1.6
W. Skyline Parkway roadwalk north end	0.4	1.4
Gogebic Creek bridge with stone canal	0.7	1.1
Power line corridor	0.7	1.1
Spirit Mountain Loop Spur south junction	1.1	0.7
Spirit Mountain Grand Avenue Chalet Trailhead	**1.8**	**0.0**

Spirit Mountain Grand Avenue Chalet Trailhead to Waseca Street Trailhead

Directions and GPS Waypoints: Northbound: Take I-35 Exit #246. Go south on Becks Rd. 4.4 miles. Turn north onto Commonwealth Ave., go 2.9 miles, turn west on Warwick St. to enter Grand Avenue Chalet parking lot. Southbound: Take I-35 Exit #251B, go 2.0 miles, turn west on Warwick St. to enter Grand Avenue Chalet parking lot. GPS: 46.715142, -92.205031

Facilities: Toilets, restaurant

Size: Large

Overnight parking: No

Winter access: Yes

Special notes: Trailhead is shared with mountain bikers, Nordic skiers, and other Spirit Mountain Recreation Area visitors. The SHT can also be accessed at the Spirit Mountain Parking Lot D Trailhead (from I-35, take Exit #249. Go south on Boundary Ave. 0.2 miles, turn east on Skyline Parkway, go 0.4 miles to parking lot on left. GPS: 46.719727, -92.218555), located on the Spirit Mountain Loop Spur.

SECTION SNAPSHOT

Trail Atlas map: A-4

Total distance: 3.2 miles (Additional 0.2-mile spur trail to Waseca Street Trailhead)

Elevation change: Most of the elevation change is gentle.

Hazards and concerns: Many rocks

Synopsis: As the Superior Hiking Trail climbs out of the Spirit Mountain Recreation Area, it follows and crosses cascading Knowlton Creek. At the northeast end of the section, the Trail follows Kingsbury Creek before crossing it on a snowmobile bridge.

▪ **Spirit Mountain Loop.** A 1.9-mile loop spur can be combined with the main Superior Hiking Trail to create a 3.5-mile loop around the Spirit Mountain Recreation Area with several convenient access points. The spur trail also passes through the Spirit Mountain Campground, a fee camping area optimally located for backpackers travelling through Duluth.

MILEAGE	Northbound	Southbound
Spirit Mountain Grand Avenue Chalet Trailhead	**0.0**	**3.4**
Spirit Mountain Loop Spur north junction	0.9	2.5
Knowlton Creek bridge	1.0	2.4
52nd Avenue Creek	1.4	2.0
Vista, bench	2.0	1.4
Spur to Waseca Street Trailhead	*3.2*	*0.2*
Waseca Street Trailhead	**3.4**	**0.0**

The Duluth SHT: A Rugged, Urban Trail Experience

Panoramic views of one of the largest working ports on the Great Lakes. There are choice vistas of not just Lake Superior but the St. Louis River Estuary and the Port of Duluth-Superior. Although pure silence is not an attribute of the Duluth SHT, the thrum of the port and the railroad yards are far below its hillside perch, offering the contrast and connection between industry and the natural resources of the Upper Midwest.

▌Waseca Street Trailhead to Skyline Parkway Trailhead

BEGINNING TRAILHEAD

Directions and GPS Waypoints: Northbound: Take I-35 Exit #251A, go on Cody St. 0.4 miles. Turn south on N. 63rd Ave. W., go 0.6 miles. Turn south on Grand Ave., go 0.7 miles. Turn west on Waseca St. go 0.2 miles to parking lot. Southbound: Take I-35 Exit #251B, go south 0.8 miles on Grand Ave., turn west on Waseca St., go 0.2 miles to parking lot. GPS: 46.727420, -92.190571

Facilities: Toilet, picnic area

Size: Small

Overnight parking: No

Winter access: No

Special notes: The trailhead is located just a few hundred yards from the Lake Superior Zoo entrance. A nearby playground offers access to seasonal public bathrooms and a picnic area.

SECTION SNAPSHOT

Trail Atlas map: A-4

Total distance: 2.1 miles (Additional 0.2-mile spur trail from Waseca Street Trailhead)

Elevation change: There is some climbing and descending along rock ridges followed by a sustained climb along Keene Creek.

Hazards and concerns: Use caution when crossing Cody Street. Pay attention to signage to stay on the Superior Hiking Trail.

Synopsis: This section features multiple encounters with the Cross City Trail, a multi-use path; a short climb along Kingsbury Creek to rocky outcrops and wide views; and many intersections with roads and bike trails. A close encounter with Keene Creek punctuates the northeastern end of this section.

MILEAGE	Northbound	Southbound
Waseca Street Trailhead	**0.0**	**2.3**
Spur from Waseca Street Trailhead	*0.2*	*2.1*
I 35 overpass	1.0	1.3
Short N. 66th Avenue W. roadwalk	1.2	1.1
Cody Street crossing	1.2	1.1
Westgate Boulevard roadwalk south end	1.2	1.1
Westgate Boulevard roadwalk north end	1.4	0.9
Railroad bridge	1.8	0.5
Overhead pipeline	2.0	0.3
Highland Street overpass	2.2	0.1
Keene Creek	2.3	0.0
Skyline Parkway Trailhead	**2.3**	**0.0**

The Duluth SHT:
A Rugged, Urban Trail Experience

Loved, but not to death. The Duluth SHT is enjoyed much by locals but rarely experiences the kind of use seen at more popular destinations up the shore. It is very possible to travel several miles without encountering another trail user. 𐤀𐤀

▌ Skyline Parkway Trailhead to Haines Road Trailhead

Directions and GPS Waypoints: Northbound: Take I-35 Exit #249. Turn north, cross bridge, turn east onto Skyline Parkway. Drive 2.4 miles, turn northeast to stay on Skyline Parkway, cross Highland St., turn south into parking lot. Southbound: Take I-35 Exit #252. Turn north, go 0.8 miles. Turn west on Highland St., go 1.1 miles, turn northeast on Skyline Parkway, turn south into parking lot. GPS: 46.750537, -92.187057

Facilities: None

Size: Medium

Overnight parking: No

Winter access: No

Special notes: This trailhead is shared with mountain bikers.

SECTION SNAPSHOT

Trail Atlas map: A-4

Total distance: 2.6 miles

Elevation change: This section features steep elevation changes on both sides of the ridgeline.

Hazards and concerns: Be careful on steep stairs near Keene Creek. Use caution when crossing Skyline Parkway. Pay attention to signage to stay on the SHT at several trail junctions.

Synopsis: After a short walk along Keene Creek, the Trail crosses Skyline Parkway and continues through woods to a ridgeline with several rocky overlooks and many viewpoints, most notably Peace Ridge. The Trail descends several switchbacks, crosses Merritt Creek, and travels through a tunnel under Haines Road. The Brewer Park Loop Spur offers an enjoyable day trip option from either end of this section.

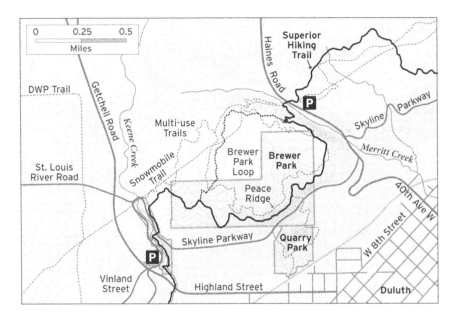

SPUR TRAIL

¡ Brewer Park Loop. This 0.9-mile spur trail through a wooded city park creates an enjoyable loop accessible from either Skyline Parkway Trailhead or Haines Road Trailhead.

MILEAGE	NORTHBOUND	SOUTHBOUND
Skyline Parkway Trailhead	**0.0**	**2.6**
Keene Creek	0.2	2.4
W. Skyline Parkway crossing	0.3	2.3
Brewer Park Loop spur west junction	0.9	1.7
Peace Ridge	1.5	1.1
Brewer Park Loop spur east junction	2.3	0.3
Tunnel under Haines Road	2.5	0.1
Spur to Haines Road Trailhead	*2.6*	*0.0*
Haines Road Trailhead	**2.6**	**0.0**

▌ Haines Road Trailhead to
North 24th Avenue West Trailhead

Directions and GPS Waypoints: Take I-35 Exit #253B, turn north on 40th Ave. W., go 1.7 miles to parking lot on right. GPS: 46.762386, -92.170095

Facilities: None

Size: Medium

Overnight parking: No

Winter access: Yes

Special notes: This trailhead is shared with mountain bikers and other users of multi-use trails in the area. It may be full during peak times, so consider having an alternate parking option in mind. A short sidewalk spur along Haines Road leads to the main Superior Hiking Trail.

SECTION SNAPSHOT

Trail Atlas maps: A-4, A-5

Total distance: 2.8 miles

Elevation change: There are steep areas on this section, primarily around Skyline Parkway.

Hazards and concerns: Use caution when crossing Skyline Parkway.

Synopsis: The Superior Hiking Trail traverses rolling hills with several rocky knob vistas before descending and crossing Skyline Parkway. After a long boardwalk through a wet area, the Trail passes through Lincoln Park and crosses Miller Creek.

MILEAGE	Northbound	Southbound
Haines Road Trailhead	**0.0**	**2.8**
Spur from Haines Road Trailhead	0.0	2.8
Power line corridor	0.8	2.0
W. Skyline Parkway crossing	1.6	1.2
N. 27th Avenue W. crossing	2.2	0.6
W. 10th Street roadwalk south end	2.2	0.6
W. 10th Street roadwalk north end	2.3	0.5
Lincoln Park Drive crossing	2.6	0.2
Miller Creek bridge	2.7	0.1
N. 24th Avenue W. crossing	2.7	0.1
N. 24th Avenue W. Trailhead	**2.8**	**0.0**

The Duluth SHT:
A Rugged, Urban Trail Experience

Sharing recreational lands, harmoniously. The SHT crosses and overlaps with several mountain bike trails that are part of the Duluth Traverse network of bike trails. Those crossings are well-marked, but in the few places the SHT is routed onto a mountain bike trail. Be alert and watch for cyclists. ⋀⋀

▊ North 24ᵗʰ Avenue West Trailhead to Rose Garden Trailhead

Directions and GPS Waypoints: Take I-35 Exit #255A, go 1.5 miles, turn south at stoplight onto Piedmont Ave., turn south onto N. 24th Ave. W., cross Skyline Parkway, and turn east into parking lot. GPS: 46.773328, -92.142340

Facilities: None

Size: Medium

Overnight parking: No

Winter access: Yes

Special notes: Additional trail access points are available in this section at Enger Park and Twin Ponds Trailhead (Take I-35 Exit #255A 1.5 miles, turn south at stoplight onto Piedmont Ave., turn south onto N. 24th Ave. W., turn east onto Skyline Parkway, go 1.5 miles to parking lot. GPS: 46.778729, -92.123071).

SECTION SNAPSHOT

Trail Atlas map: A-5

Total distance: 5.4 miles

Elevation change: There is a significant descent from Enger Tower down to Canal Park. The Trail between Canal Park and the Rose Garden is likely the flattest area along the Superior Hiking Trail.

Hazards and concerns: Use caution at several road crossings.

Synopsis: The most urban section of the Superior Hiking Trail features encounters with the historic Enger Tower, the Minnesota Slip Bridge, the famed Aerial Lift Bridge in Canal Park Business District, and the shores of Lake Superior on the Duluth Lakewalk.

MILEAGE	Northbound	Southbound
N. 24th Avenue W. Trailhead	**0.0**	**5.4**
Skyline Parkway overpass	0.0	5.4
Forgotten Park	0.3	5.1
Hank Jansen Drive crossing	0.8	4.6
Short Enger Tower Drive roadwalk	1.0	4.4
American-Japanese Peace Bell in Enger Park	1.2	4.2
Spur to Twin Ponds Trailhead	*1.4*	*4.0*
W. Skyline Parkway crossing	1.4	4.0
W. 3rd Street crossing	1.8	3.6
W. Michigan Street crossing and sidewalk south end	2.2	3.2
W. Michigan Street sidewalk north end	2.3	3.1
Interstate 35 footbridge	2.3	3.1
Railroad crossing	2.5	2.9
Minnesota Slip Bridge	3.3	2.1
Aerial Lift Bridge	3.6	1.8
Duluth Lakewalk west end	3.7	1.7
Duluth Lakewalk east end	5.1	0.3
Rose Garden Trailhead	**5.4**	**0.0**

Rose Garden Trailhead to Hartley Nature Center Trailhead

Directions and GPS Waypoints: Take I-35 Exit #258, turn north on 21st Ave. E., go 200 feet to London Road. Turn west on London Rd. at traffic light, go 7 blocks to parking lot on left. GPS: 46.798732, -92.079603

Facilities: None

Size: Medium

Overnight parking: No

Winter access: Yes

Special notes: Three-hour limit at Rose Garden parking area. Additional access points are available in this section at Chester Bowl Trailhead (Take I-35 exit #256A, continue northeast on Mesaba Ave., go 1.3 miles to E Skyline Parkway. Turn east on E Skyline Parkway, go 1.4 miles, then turn west onto Chester Park Dr. to parking lot. GPS: 46.813031, -92.092515).

SECTION SNAPSHOT

Trail Atlas maps: A-5, A-6

Total distance: 4.4 miles

Elevation change: A long but fairly gentle climb from the Rose Garden through Chester Park. There are a couple of steep stairways on the northern half of this section.

Hazards and concerns: Use caution at road crossings and on roadwalks.

Synopsis: From the Rose Garden, the Superior Hiking Trail ascends to the Chester Creek gorge and travels along and above the scenic creek and its waterfalls. The Trail passes through the heart of the University of Minnesota campus en route to Bagley Nature Area and a unique viewing platform at the top of Rock Hill. Inside Hartley Park, the Trail climbs to several seasonal viewpoints, then descends again to pass Hartley Pond and Hartley Nature Center.

Pro tip: There are abundant opportunities for loops and extended adventures using the many hiking and multi-use trails that connect Chester Park, Bagley Nature Area, and Hartley Park.

SPUR TRAILS

- **Bagley Nature Area Campground.** This 0.4-mile spur trail leads into the heart of Bagley Nature Area with a small campground. Sites may be reserved ahead of time or available on a walk-in basis, and payment is required.
- **Rock Knob.** Near Hartley Pond, this 0.3-mile spur trail ascends to the top of a scenic peak.

MILEAGE	Northbound	Southbound
Rose Garden Trailhead	**0.0**	**4.4**
London Road crossing	0.1	4.3
S. 14th Avenue E. sidewalk south end	0.1	4.3
N. 14th Avenue E. sidewalk north end	0.4	4.0
E. 4th Street crossing, Chester Park boundary	0.4	4.0
E. 9th Street overpass	1.3	3.1
Chester Bowl Trailhead	1.4	3.0
N. 19th Avenue E. crossing	1.6	2.8
W. College Street crossing	1.6	2.8
Junction Avenue sidewalk south end	1.6	2.8
Junction Avenue sidewalk north end, crossing	2.0	2.4
Bagley Nature Area viewing platform	2.2	2.2
Spur to Bagley Nature Area fee campground	*2.5*	*1.9*
W. Arrowhead Road crossing	2.7	1.7
Old Hartley Road junction	3.0	1.4
Spur to Rock Knob	*4.0*	*0.4*
Spillway bridge	4.1	0.3
Hartley Nature Center Trailhead	**4.4**	**0.0**

▌ Hartley Nature Center Trailhead to Martin Road Trailhead

Directions and GPS Waypoints: Take I-35 Exit #258, turn north on 21st Ave. E., go 0.7 miles. Turn north on Woodland Ave., go 2.6 miles. Turn west on Hartley Nature Center driveway to parking lot. GPS: 46.838725, -92.081437

Facilities: Toilet

Size: Large

Overnight parking: No

Winter access: Yes

Special notes: Trailhead is shared with other visitors to the park and Hartley Nature Center.

SECTION SNAPSHOT

Trail Atlas map: A-6

Total distance: 3.0 miles

Elevation change: This is a very gentle section with large parts on roads.

Hazards and concerns: Use caution at road crossings and on roadwalks.

Synopsis: The Superior Hiking Trail leaves Hartley Nature Center and follows a mix of trail, sidewalk, and roadwalk through quaint Duluth neighborhoods and between cemeteries. A highlight of the section is the cliffside vista above Amity Creek as the Trail passes through Downer Park.

Pro tip: Hartley Nature Center, an independent nonprofit organization, offers snowshoe and Nordic ski rentals in the winter and programs for the general public throughout the year focused on a wide range of natural history topics.

MILEAGE	Northbound	Southbound
Hartley Nature Center Trailhead	**0.0**	**3.0**
Woodland Avenue sidewalk west end	0.2	2.8
Woodland Ave sidewalk east end, crossing	0.4	2.6
Carlisle Avenue roadwalk west end	0.4	2.6
Carlisle Avenue roadwalk east end	0.7	2.3
Vermilion Road roadwalk south end	0.7	2.3
Vermilion Road roadwalk north end	1.6	1.4
Pleasant View Road crossing	2.5	0.5
Martin Road Trailhead	**3.0**	**0.0**

The Duluth SHT:
A Rugged, Urban Trail Experience

A few things to note about the Duluth SHT:

• Winter use is ideal: The Trail is well-packed by snowshoers, hikers, and runners all winter long. Snowshoes are not always needed to enjoy the Duluth SHT.

• Watch out for "social trails": Neighborhood residents come and go from the SHT on informal trails. Watch for blue blazes and SHT signs to keep on the Trail.

• The Duluth SHT may best be enjoyed in combination with other Duluth amenities. Take advantage of the city's offerings, from the fine shops in the Lincoln Park Craft District and Canal Park to the restaurants, lodges, and other recreational opportunities that make Duluth a regional destination. ⋀⋏

Martin Road Trailhead to Lake County Road 301 Trailhead

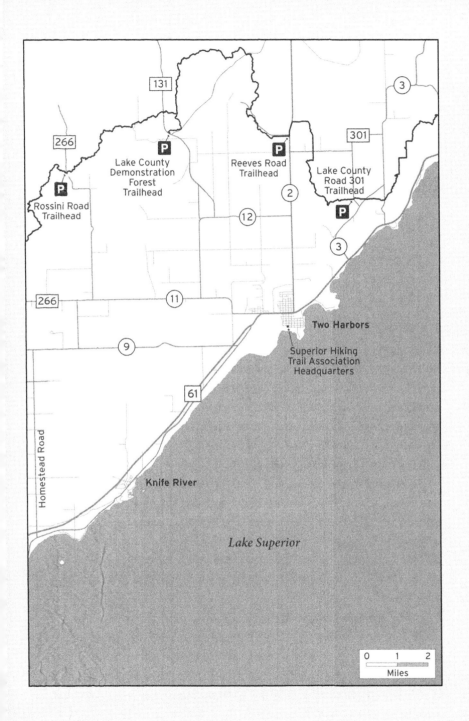

Martin Road Trailhead to
Lake County Road 301 Trailhead

▌ Overview

Leaving the urban sections of the Superior Hiking Trail south of **Martin Road Trailhead,** the Trail wanders through actively-managed forest and past several small ponds. The Trail often affords a pleasant open feeling, particularly along the southern parts of this segment, where the Trail shares the route of the North Shore State Trail (NSST). There is an impressive bridge over the Lester River before the Trail winds through cedars on its way to Lismore Road.

After a short walk alongside **Lismore Road** and crossing Jean Duluth Road, the Superior Hiking Trail heads back into the woods to the wide North Shore State Trail, where the broad path is ideal for appreciating wildflowers and spotting wildlife. A giant white pine is a reminder to follow signage carefully; the Trail veers off the NSST here on its way through low-lying terrain. As the Trail nears Normanna Road, it shares the route of the NSST once again.

From **Normanna Road Trailhead,** a short spur trail connects to the main Superior Hiking Trail. The Trail passes a series of beaver ponds before climbing to a hill in a managed forest. In addition to the joy of watching forests regenerate, the beauty of the Sucker River is a highlight of this section. A spur trail to the Western Fox Farm Road Trailhead leads to an overlook of the area and a long descent.

The spur trail from **Western Fox Farm Road Trailhead** ascends steadily after crossing the Sucker River. The Superior Hiking Trail passes multiple forestry kiosks in this section, skirts the edge of Fox Farm Pond, and passes through several open areas. The Trail crosses the North Shore State Trail several times.

From the **Eastern Fox Farm Road Trailhead,** the Superior Hiking Trail continues through forests managed by Saint Louis County, encounters the West Branch of the Knife River multiple times, travels through moose-inhabited woods near beaver ponds, and ascends to seasonal views of Lake Superior and legacy pines. A descent to Rossini Road features the noteworthy, but perhaps slightly underwhelming 12 Mile View.

From **Rossini Road Trailhead,** the Superior Hiking Trail crosses several creeks and passes ponds on gentle terrain. McCarthy Creek Falls, a highlight of this section, varies in size and waterflow depending on the season. The rocky path crosses a small stream and the Drummond Grade before climbing to a spur trail to the Lake County Demonstration Forest Trailhead and trail network.

A spur trail from the **Lake County Demonstration Forest Trailhead** traverses the Demonstration Forest en route to the main Superior Hiking Trail. Moderately scenic Wholly Hill and the undeniably scenic West Branch of the Stewart River are two of the highlights in this rolling section. Underneath elevated railroad tracks, thousands of tiny taconite pellets carpet the Trail, a clue to one of the industrial strongholds of the region. Reeves Falls, a small but pretty waterfall, can be found on the campsite spur trail, but it may dry up by the end of summer. After several crossings, the Trail follows Reeves Road to its trailhead adjacent to Highway 2.

The **Reeves Road Trailhead** brings the Superior Hiking Trail to a brief roadwalk on Highway 2, after which the Trail joins a snowmobile trail across private property. This section claims the highest density of private lands anywhere on the Trail. Tread lightly and gratefully across this area. A steep, rocky descent and a crossing of Gun Club Road come shortly before the Trail follows Silver Creek off-and-on, before veering away from the creek toward the Lake County Road 301 Trailhead. ⋀⋀

Martin Road Trailhead to Lismore Road

Directions and GPS Waypoints: Take I-35 Exit #258, turn north on 21st Ave. E., go 0.7 miles. Turn north on Woodland Ave., go 1.2 miles. Turn east on Snively Rd., go 1.0 miles to intersection with Jean Duluth Rd. Continue on Jean Duluth Rd. 1.9 miles. Turn west on Martin Rd., go 1.2 miles to parking lot on left. GPS: 46.865322, -92.070977

Facilities: Toilet, trail register

Size: Large

Overnight parking: Allowed

Winter access: Yes

Special notes: Trailhead is shared with North Shore State Trail (NSST) users and may be closed in spring during wet conditions.

SECTION SNAPSHOT

Trail Atlas maps: B-1, B-2

Total distance: 6.8 miles

Elevation change: Very minimal. This is among the flattest sections of the Superior Hiking Trail.

SHT campsites: Two

Hazards and concerns: There are several road crossings, including a short roadwalk along and crossing of Martin Road. Be aware of other users on the multi-use North Shore State Trail, particularly in winter.

Synopsis: This is a relatively easy section that partially shares the route of the North Shore State Trail. It features several ponds and crossings over Amity Creek and Lester River.

Pro tip: The NSST can be damp during spring and is not regularly mowed during the summer.

SPUR TRAIL

▪ **Del's Pond.** This short spur trail leads to the shore of this lovely pond—a great place to view wildlife.

CAMPSITES

▲ **Bald Eagle Campsite**
Size: Small
Water source: Beaver pond
Campsite features a view of the pond and a trail register.
53.1 ⊖ ⊙ 1.2, 6.7

▲ **White Pine Campsite**
Size: Medium
Water source: Lester River
Campsite sits above the river in a cluster of pines.
54.3, 1.2 ⊖ ⊙ 5.5, 9.2

MILEAGE	Northbound	Southbound
Martin Road Trailhead	**0.0**	**6.8**
Vermilion Road crossing, Martin Road roadwalk, west end	0.1	6.7
Martin Road roadwalk, east end	0.3	6.5
North Shore State Trail south end	0.5	6.3
E. Branch Amity Creek bridge		
Riley Road crossing	1.0	5.8
W. Tischer Road crossing	1.8	5
Prindle Road crossing	2.3	4.5
North Shore State Trail north end	2.9	3.9
Spur to Del's Pond	*3.7*	*3.1*
Spur to Bald Eagle Campsite	*4.8*	*2.0*
Spur to White Pine Campsite	*6.0*	*0.8*
Brief overlap with North Shore State Trail, Lester River bridge, shelter	6.1	0.7
Lismore Road No trailhead. *Check errata for updates.*	**6.8**	**0.0**

▊ Lismore Road to Normanna Road Trailhead

Special notes: At the time of writing, there is no Superior Hiking Trail trailhead at Lismore Road. Check the Trail Conditions page on the Superior Hiking Trail Association website for more up-to-date information. Please respect adjacent private property and make sure to stay on the Trail.

SECTION SNAPSHOT

Trail Atlas map: B-2

Total distance: 6.8 miles (Additional 0.1-mile spur trail to Normanna Road Trailhead)

Elevation change: This is one of the flattest sections of the Superior Hiking Trail.

SHT campsites: One

Hazards and concerns: There are some road crossings, most notably Jean Duluth Road. Be aware of other users on the multi-use North Shore State Trail, particularly in winter.

Synopsis: This is a gentle section that shares the North Shore State Trail for a couple of miles and features crossings over Harvey Creek and French River.

CAMPSITE

▲ **Lone Tree Campsite**
 Size: Small
 Water source: Harvey Creek, located just north of the campsite
 Campsite is near an open area great for stargazing.
 6.7, 5.5 ⊙ ⊙ 3.7, 7.7

MILEAGE	Northbound	Southbound
Lismore Road		
No trailhead. *Check errata for updates.*	**0.0**	**6.9**
Lonely Pine Drive crossing	0.1	6.8
Jean Duluth Road crossing	0.6	6.3
North Shore State Trail south end	0.9	6.0
North Shore State Trail north end	3.7	3.2
Lone Tree Campsite	4.7	2.2
Harvey Creek	4.8	2.1
North Shore State Trail south end	6.0	0.9
N. Tischer Road crossing		
Normanna Road crossing	6.5	0.4
French River bridge	6.8	0.1
North Shore State Trail north end, spur to Normanna Road Trailhead	*6.8*	*0.1*
Normanna Road Trailhead	***6.9***	***0.0***

▌ Normanna Road Trailhead to Western Fox Farm Road Trailhead

Directions and GPS Waypoints: Take I-35 Exit #258, turn north on 21st Ave. E., go 0.7 miles. Turn north on Woodland Ave., go 1.2 miles. Turn east on Snively Rd., go 1.4 miles to intersection with Jean Duluth Rd. Continue on Jean Duluth Rd. 9.8 miles. Turn east on Normanna Rd., go 1.0 mile, turn east to stay on Normanna Rd., go 1.6 miles. Turn north into driveway for parking lot. GPS: 46.982799, -91.995139

Facilities: Toilet, kiosk

Size: Medium

Overnight parking: Allowed

Winter access: Yes

Special notes: Trailhead is shared with North Shore State Trail snowmobile users.

SECTION SNAPSHOT

Trail Atlas maps: B-2, B-3

Total distance: 8.1 miles (Additional 0.1-mile spur trail from Normanna Road Trailhead, 0.9-mile spur trail to Western Fox Farm Road Trailhead)

Elevation change: While this section features more elevation change than the preceding sections, it is still very gentle with only a couple of sustained climbs.

SHT campsites: Two

Hazards and concerns: There are several junctions with other trail networks in this section.

Synopsis: A tour of beaver ponds and actively-managed forests, including a few "rendez-views" of and with the Sucker River.

Pro tip: Trail between Normanna Road Trailhead and Heron Pond Campsite is a favorite for snowshoeing.

■ **Western Fox Farm Road Trailhead.** Spur trail leads 0.9 miles downhill, crossing the Sucker River on an A-frame bridge and arriving at the Western Fox Farm Road Trailhead.

CAMPSITES

▲ **Heron Pond Campsite**
Size: Medium
Water source: Nearby pond
Campsite features semi-private tent pads and excellent wildlife viewing.
9.2, 3.7 ⊙ ⊙ 4.0, 6.7

▲ **Sucker River Campsite**
Size: Medium
Water source: Sucker River
Tall pines with minimal undergrowth give this campsite an open feel.
7.7, 4.0 ⊙ ⊙ 2.7, 10.0

MILEAGE	Northbound	Southbound
Normanna Road Trailhead	**0.0**	**9.1**
Spur from Normanna Road Trailhead	*0.1*	*9.0*
North Shore State Trail crossings	0.3	8.8
Heron Pond Campsite	1.7	7.4
Bridge	2.6	6.5
Reservoir Road crossing, gated	2.6	6.5
Sucker River Campsite	5.7	3.4
Brief junction with North Shore State Trail, bridge, shelter	6.9	2.2
Spur to western Fox Farm Road Trailhead	*8.2*	*0.9*
Western Fox Farm Road Trailhead	**9.1**	**0.0**

Western Fox Farm Road Trailhead to Eastern Fox Farm Road Trailhead

Directions and GPS Waypoints: Take I-35 Exit #258, turn north on 21st Ave. E., go 0.7 miles. Turn north on Woodland Ave., go 1.2 miles. Turn east on Snively Rd., go 1.4 miles to intersection with Jean Duluth Rd. Continue on Jean Duluth Rd. 9.8 miles. Turn east on Normanna Rd., go 1.0 mile, continue onto Pequaywan Lake Rd. 4.3 miles. Slight turn east onto Fox Farm Rd., go 3.2 miles to parking lot on right. GPS: 47.043111, -91.919982

Facilities: None

Size: Small

Overnight parking: Allowed

Winter access: No

Special notes: Be aware there are two Superior Hiking Trail trailheads on Fox Farm Road. Western Fox Farm Road Trailhead has also gone by the nickname "Sucker River Trailhead."

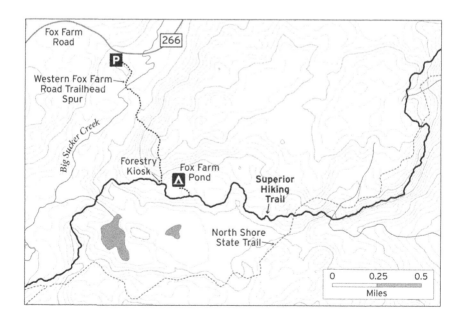

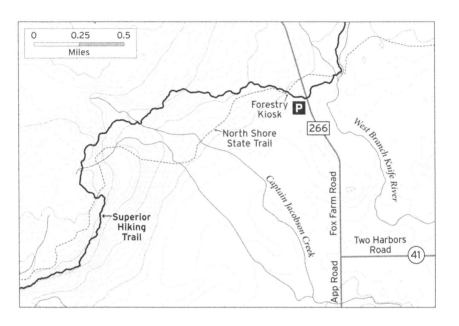

Trail Atlas maps: B-3, B-4

Total distance: 4.0 miles (Additional 0.9-mile spur trail from Western Fox Farm Road Trailhead)

Elevation change: The most dramatic climb is on the spur trail from Western Fox Farm Road Trailhead to the main Superior Hiking Trail. From there, the Trail frequently rises and falls but without particularly challenging elevation changes.

SHT campsites: One

Synopsis: After crossing a bridge over the Sucker River along a spur trail from the trailhead to the main Superior Hiking Trail, the route travels through actively-managed forests and past Fox Farm Pond.

Pro tip: There are several crossings with the North Shore State Trail that enable users to enjoy a long loop by using both trails.

- **Western Fox Farm Road Trailhead.** Spur trail leads 0.9 miles uphill, crosses the Sucker River on an A-frame bridge, and arrives at the main Superior Hiking Trail near Fox Farm Pond.

▲ **Fox Farm Pond Campsite**
Size: Medium
Water source: Small beaver pond, stagnant by late summer
Campsite frequently has reports of distant coyotes singing.
6.7, 2.7 ← → 7.3, 13.4

MILEAGE	Northbound	Southbound
Western Fox Farm Road Trailhead	**0.0**	**4.9**
Spur from western Fox Farm Road Trailhead	*0.9*	*4.0*
Forestry kiosk, register	0.9	4.0
Fox Farm Pond Campsite	1.1	3.8
North Shore State Trail crossing	1.9	3.0
North Shore State Trail crossing	3.1	1.8
Forestry kiosk	4.4	0.5
North Shore State Trail crossing	4.8	0.1
Eastern Fox Farm Road Trailhead	**4.9**	**0.0**

A Public Forest Primer

At this point in the journey on the Superior Hiking Trail, a primer on public forests is in order. The SHT throughout its course is almost solely due to the existence of public land. This is land owned by citizens and managed by counties, the state of Minnesota, and the federal government.

These lands are managed for public benefit, as revenue generated from timber harvests supports county, state, and federal governments. Timber plays a vital role in the region's economy and helps keep these lands in public ownership. In essence, trees on this land are a crop harvested periodically, generating revenues for those governments. Managed by St. Louis and Lake counties, the forests in these SHT sections are in various stages of regeneration, from recently logged land to forests of aspen and white spruce that are shady, verdant, and mature—and ready for another cut.

The forests produce consumer products, like lumber and pulp for paper-making, that we all use. In addition, commercial harvests play a vital role in maintaining forest vigor. These activities along the SHT can be inconvenient for Trail users at times: the Trail can be obscured by downed trees and brush, the tread of the Trail may be damaged (temporarily) by machines, and the esthetics of a recently harvested landscape can look a bit post-apocalyptic. But what might appear as an empty landscape is actually a young forest at an early stage of the larger lifecycle of a sustainably managed natural resource. Both counties, in cooperation with the SHTA, have posted educational kiosks throughout these sections with photos highlighting the regeneration over the years. ⋀⋀

Eastern Fox Farm Road Trailhead to Rossini Road Trailhead

Directions and GPS Waypoints: At MN-61 milepost 14.9, turn north on Homestead Rd., go 5.75 miles. Turn west on W. Knife River Rd., go 0.5 miles. Turn north on App Rd., go 1.5 miles to intersection. App Rd. changes to Fox Farm Rd. at this intersection. Continue north on Fox Farm Rd. 0.9 miles to parking lot on left. GPS: 47.044753, -91.861366

Facilities: None

Size: Small

Overnight parking: Allowed

Winter access: Yes

Special notes: Trailhead is shared with North Shore State Trail users.

SECTION SNAPSHOT

Trail Atlas map: B-4

Total distance: 6.4 miles

Elevation change: There are several climbs on this section, including Fox Farm Hill, but it is still one of the easier sections of the Superior Hiking Trail.

SHT campsites: One

Synopsis: Highlights of this section include encounters with the West Branch of the Knife River, a large beaver pond, and a view of Lake Superior from 12 Mile View.

CAMPSITE

▲ **Big Bend Campsite**
Size: Medium
Water source: West Branch of the Knife River
Remote campsite often has moose signs nearby.
10.0, 7.3 ⊙ ⊙ 6.1, 7.2

MILEAGE	Northbound	Southbound
Eastern Fox Farm Road Trailhead	**0.0**	**6.4**
Fox Farm Road crossing	0.0	6.4
Brief junction with North Shore State Trail, bridge	0.3	6.1
Fox Farm Hill	1.5	4.9
West Branch Knife River bridge	3.1	3.3
Big Bend Campsite	3.5	2.9
Beaver pond	4.0	2.4
12 Mile View	5.9	0.5
Rossini Road Trailhead	**6.4**	**0.0**

Rossini Road Trailhead to Lake County Demonstration Forest Trailhead

BEGINNING TRAILHEAD

Directions and GPS Waypoints: At MN-61 milepost 14.9, turn north on Homestead Rd., go 5.75 miles. Turn east on W. Knife River Rd., go 1.4 miles. Turn north on Culbertson Rd., go 1.5 miles. Turn east on Two Harbors Rd., go 0.5 miles. Turn north on Laine Rd., go 3.5 miles. Turn west on Rossini Rd., go 1.3 miles to parking lot on left. GPS: 47.090624, -91.821154

Facilities: None

Size: Small

Overnight parking: Allowed

Winter access: No

Special notes: Trailhead is often inaccessible in early spring due to muddy conditions.

SECTION SNAPSHOT

Trail Atlas map: B-5

Total distance: 5.6 miles (Additional 1.2-mile spur trail to Lake County Demonstration Forest Trailhead)

Elevation change: This is a gentle section with a few climbs of around 100 feet.

SHT campsites: Two

Synopsis: Section features relatively flat terrain, several small creeks including a waterfall at McCarthy Creek, and signs of historic railroads and mining.

SPUR TRAIL

▪ **Lake County Demonstration Forest Trailhead.** A 1.2-mile spur trail leads primarily downhill from the main Superior Hiking Trail, at times sharing trails from the Lake County Demonstration Forest network. The spur trail arrives at the trailhead where there is an outhouse, shelter, and parking available.

CAMPSITES

▲ **McCarthy Creek Campsite**
Size: Small
Water source: McCarthy Creek
Very small campsite is not appropriate for large group use. It is located near a waterfall and a trail register.
13.4, 6.1 ⊕ ⊖ 1.1, 6.6

▲ **Ferguson Campsite**
Size: Small
Water source: A small tributary of Knife River, located just south of the campsite
Campsite is on a hill above the tributary.
7.2, 1.1 ⊕ ⊖ 5.5, 9.5

MILEAGE	Northbound	Southbound
Rossini Road Trailhead	**0.0**	**6.8**
Rossini Road crossing	0.0	6.8
Power line corridor	0.9	5.9
Pond	2.3	4.5
McCarthy Creek Campsite, register	3.2	3.6
McCarthy Creek waterfall	3.2	3.6
Epic tree stand	3.4	3.4
Old Drummond Road crossing	4.0	2.8
Ferguson Campsite	4.3	2.5
Lake County Road 131 crossing, short roadwalk	5.0	1.8
Mining test pit	5.1	1.7
Spur to Lake County Demonstration Forest Trailhead	*5.6*	*1.2*
Lake County Demonstration Forest Trailhead	**6.8**	**0.0**

Lake County Demonstration Forest Trailhead to Reeves Road Trailhead

Directions and GPS Waypoints: At MN-61 milepost 23.8, turn west onto Stanley Road, cross southbound MN-61, turn north on Shoreview Road, go 2.4 miles. Turn north on Lake County Road 12, go 2.4 miles. Turn northwest on Moen Road, go 1.1 miles. Moen Road becomes Drummond Grade, continue 2.0 miles to parking lot on right. GPS: 47.107298, -91.748713

Facilities: Toilet, kiosk, shelter, and picnic area

Size: Medium

Overnight parking: Allowed

Winter access: Yes

Special notes: Trailhead is shared with other users of the Lake County Demonstration Forest multi-use trails.

SECTION SNAPSHOT

Trail Atlas maps: B-5, B-6

Total distance: 9.7 miles (Additional 1.2-mile spur trail from Lake County Demonstration Forest Trailhead)

Elevation change: The most prolonged climb of the section is found on the spur trail from the Lake County Demonstration Forest. The Superior Hiking Trail is rolling with a few steep areas but predominantly gentle terrain.

SHT campsites: Two

Hazards and concerns: There is a known poison ivy area marked with a sign. Use caution on a 0.5-mile roadwalk along Reeves Road.

Synopsis: A long, relatively level section marked by current and historic railroads and the Stewart River.

Pro tip: Enjoy a variety of loop options using the multi-purpose trails at the Lake County Demonstration Forest.

SPUR TRAIL

■ **Lake County Demonstration Forest Trailhead.** A 1.2-mile spur trail leads primarily downhill from the main Superior Hiking Trail, at times sharing trails from the Lake County Demonstration Forest network.

CAMPSITES

▲ **Stewart River Campsite**
Size: Medium
Water source: Stewart River
Campsite has a trail register and, while not large, is a better option
for group use than other nearby campsites.
6.6, 5.5 ⊕ ⊕ 5.7, 9.7

▲ **Reeves Falls Campsite**
Size: Small
Water source: An unreliable creek which features a seasonal waterfall
Despite signage, this campsite can be easy to miss due to being lo-
cated near an overlap with Reeves Road.
9.5, 4.0 ⊕ ⊕ 5.7, 14.1

MILEAGE	Northbound	Southbound
Lake County Demonstration Forest Trailhead	*0.0*	*11.4*
Spur from Lake County Demonstration Forest Trailhead	*1.2*	*10.2*
Glacial erratic	2.6	8.8
Historic railroad cut	4.5	6.9
Stewart River Campsite, register	5.4	6.0
North Shore State Trail west end	6.5	4.9
North Shore State Trail east end	6.6	4.8
Poison ivy area	8.7	2.7
Reeves Road crossing	9.4	2.0
Reeves Falls Campsite	9.4	2.0
Reeves Road crossing	9.6	1.8
Power line corridor	10.3	1.1
Gate	10.4	1.0
Reeves Road roadwalk west end	10.9	0.5
Reeves Road roadwalk east end	11.4	0.0
Reeves Road Trailhead	**11.4**	**0.0**

Reeves Road Trailhead to Lake County Road 301 Trailhead

Directions and GPS Waypoints: At MN-61 milepost 26.0, turn north on Hwy. 2 , go 5.5 miles. Turn left on Reeves Rd., take left into parking lot. GPS: 47.105312, -91.668021

Facilities: None

Size: Medium

Overnight parking: Allowed

Winter access: Unlikely

Special notes: Trailhead can get very muddy during spring or after large rain events.

SECTION SNAPSHOT

Trail Atlas maps: B-6, B-7

Total distance: 5.4 miles

Elevation change: Mostly flat other than a rocky descent just north of Gun Club Road.

SHT campsites: One

Hazards and concerns: Use caution on 0.5-mile roadwalk along Minnesota Highway 2 and at a small rock cliff.

Synopsis: After a short roadwalk, the Superior Hiking Trail travels through woods and climbs down a steep rock cliff on stone steps. The Trail follows Silver Creek, veering away and onto a brief snowmobile trail overlap before rejoining the creek.

Pro tip: This section has one of the highest concentrations of private lands along the Superior Hiking Trail. Please be respectful.

▲ **Silver Creek Campsite**

Size: Medium

Water source: Silver Creek. Even in dry conditions there are often pools of water in the creek.

Campsite is located on public land but near many parcels of private land. Please use extra care to leave it better than you found it.

9.7, 5.7 ⊖ ⊕ 8.4, 11.6

MILEAGE	Northbound	Southbound
Reeves Road Trailhead	**0.0**	**4.9**
Minnesota Highway 2 roadwalk south end	0.0	4.9
Minnesota Highway 2 roadwalk north end	0.5	4.4
Rock cliff	1.3	3.6
Gun Club Road crossing	1.5	3.4
Silver Creek Campsite	3.7	1.2
Small bridge	4.6	0.0
Lake County Road 301 Trailhead	**4.9**	**0.0**

Lake County Road 301 Trailhead to Minnesota Highway 1 Trailhead

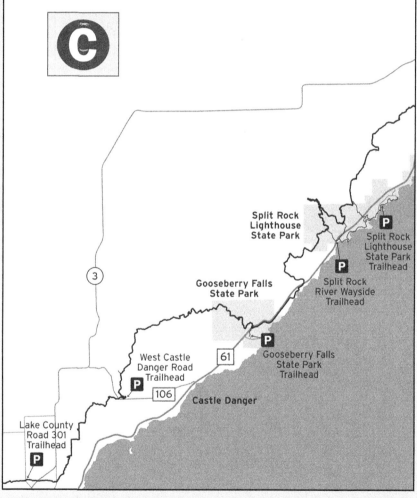

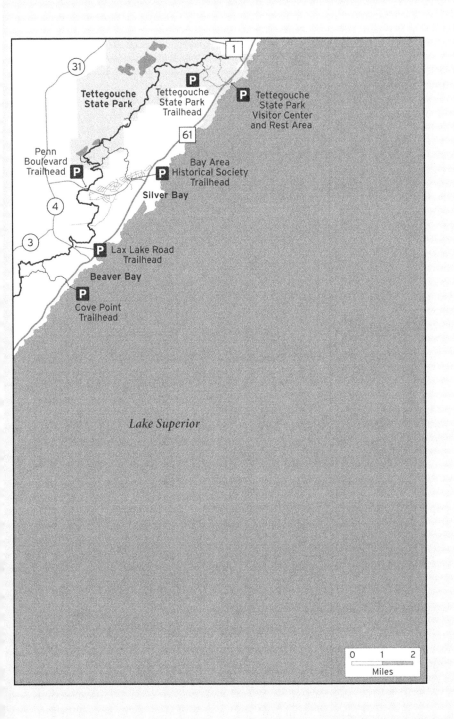

Lake County Road 301 Trailhead to Minnesota Highway 1 Trailhead

▌Overview

Lake County Road 301 Trailhead (Fors Road) was, in the early years of the Superior Hiking Trail, the southern terminus. Heading northeast, the Trail winds through an engaging section across many parcels of private land. Without the generosity of private landowners, views like Pine Ridge Overlook would be inaccessible. Several unbridged water crossings are in this section: Little Wilson Creek, the Encampment River and, after descending from a fantastic overlook, Crow Creek. These water crossings are unnoteworthy trickles for much of the year and usually passable except during snowmelt season or after a large rain event, at which point they become very flashy - running high and fast, but draining within a short period. A steep ascent past a rare poison ivy patch brings the Trail to a crossing of West Castle Danger Road and shortly thereafter, to the next trailhead.

The Superior Hiking Trail passes through **West Castle Danger Road Trailhead**. A rocky, steep ascent to Wolf Rock offers stunning views of Lake Superior and the Crow Creek Valley. Sharp-eyed trail users can see the rock outcropping where the Trail is located south of Crow Creek. A spur trail leads to an inland view while the main Superior Hiking Trail continues through deep forest before popping out at Mike's Rock Vista. The Trail descends to a long stretch along the Gooseberry River, meeting up with the trail network in Gooseberry Falls State Park, a bridge at Fifth Falls, and continuing to a bridge under Highway 61 where a spur trail leads to the heart of Gooseberry Falls State Park and a trailhead.

Gooseberry Falls State Park Visitor Center Trailhead connects to the Superior Hiking Trail with a short spur trail. The current route of the Superior Hiking Trail may soon change in this area (see sidebar The Gooseberry Gap: A Cautionary Tale). It currently shares the paved Gitchi-Gami State Trail heading northeast out of Gooseberry Falls State Park until a signed turn across Highway 61 and up Blueberry Hill Road. This dirt road leads to a junction where the Trail heads back into the woods on footpath. The Trail climbs to expansive views from Breadloaf Ridge and eventually enters Split Rock Lighthouse State Park.

Split Rock River Wayside Trailhead is a popular trailhead offering access to Lake Superior. A spur trail connects to the main Superior Hiking Trail near Strand Creek Falls. This area is one of the most well-known places along the Superior Hiking Trail. For the foreseeable future, visitors must hop across rocks or get their feet wet to cross the river along the main Trail (use extreme caution if crossing the river; a bridged crossing near Highway 61 is available when river levels are unsafe). See sidebar Future of the Split Rock River Loop for more background on this area. After following the river upstream to the crossing and back downstream, the Trail arrives at a vista of Lake Superior and the valley carved by the Split Rock River. The Trail continues along a ridgeline with glimpses of the Split Rock Lighthouse before meeting up with the historic path of the Merrill Grade logging railroad. The Trail climbs to Chapins Ridge, Christmas Tree Ridge, and Fault Line Ridge, undulating between beaver ponds and rocky outcrops with wide views. At a junction with the Cove Point Loop, views turn inland to Fault Line Valley before a long descent towards Lax Lake Road

From **Lax Lake Road Trailhead,** the Superior Hiking Trail follows a multi-use path across the Beaver River before turning downstream on a narrow, foot travel-only route. The Beaver River grows more dramatic, offering large rocks on its banks for rest. The Trail passes through old-growth white pine forests and briefly shares the Gitchi-Gami State Trail. Several parcels here are owned by Northshore Mining, and nearby signs of Minnesota's iron industry are a reminder that civilization is near. A steep climb affords nice views from rock outcroppings before descending into the City of Silver Bay.

Penn Boulevard Trailhead in Silver Bay is the gateway to one of the most popular destinations on the Superior Hiking Trail: the Bean and Bear Lakes Loop. The terrain is rocky and rooty entering Tettegouche State Park, with vistas of Silver Bay, inland ponds, and eventually Bean Lake and Bear Lake. Once off the loop portion of this section, there are dramatic inland views of Palisade Valley, Round Mountain, and Mount Trudee. A short spur leads to the worthwhile Round Mountain Mini-Loop. The SHT ascends Mount Trudee, one of the most notable landmarks of the entire Superior Hiking Trail. The Tettegouche State Park trail network offers many opportunities for further exploration and most intersections have an up-to-date map. The Trail enters the core of Tettegouche State Park as it winds towards a bridge over the Baptism River near the High Falls. A final climb meets up with a short spur trail to the Minnesota Highway 1 Trailhead. ∧∧

Lake County Road 301 Trailhead to West Castle Danger Road Trailhead

Directions and GPS Waypoints: At MN-61 milepost 28.5, turn north on Lake Co. Rd. 3, go 2.0 miles. Turn north on Lake Co. Rd. 301, and go 0.3 miles to parking lot on left. GPS: 47.076349, -91.625132

Facilities: None

Size: Small

Overnight parking: Allowed

Winter access: Yes

Special notes: This trailhead is located on private property. Please use extra care to leave it better than you found it. If the small parking lot is full, do not park along the road—please find another place to recreate.

SECTION SNAPSHOT

Trail Atlas map: C-1

Total distance: 6.0 miles

Elevation change: Relatively minimal, but there are a couple of steep elevation changes, especially near Crow Creek.

SHT campsites: None

Hazards and concerns: This section has cliffs and unbridged water crossings.

Synopsis: A changing climate is apparent in this section, where recent dramatic water events have shaped the terrain and route of the SHT. A couple of stunning overlooks showcase the surrounding landscape.

Pro tip: This section is closed before and during firearms deer hunting season each year by request of private landowners in this section; check the SHT Trail Conditions page for up-do-date information on hunting closures.

MILEAGE	Northbound	Southbound
Lake County Road 301 Trailhead	**0.0**	**6.0**
Stream crossing	0.1	5.9
Highway 3 crossing	0.4	5.6
Little Wilson Creek crossing	0.5	5.5
Loop Road crossing	1.1	4.9
Ridgeline Road crossing	1.5	4.5
Pine Ridge Overlook	2.1	3.9
Register, Encampment River crossing	3.4	2.3
Crow Creek crossing	5.7	0.3
Poison ivy area near stairs	5.7	0.3
West Castle Danger Road crossing	5.8	0.2
West Castle Danger Road Trailhead	**6.0**	**0.0**

West Castle Danger Road Trailhead to Gooseberry Falls State Park Visitor Center Trailhead

BEGINNING TRAILHEAD

Directions and GPS Waypoints: At MN-61 milepost 36.6, turn west on W. Castle Danger Rd., go 2.4 miles to parking lot on right. GPS: 47.112691, -91.557208

Facilities: None

Size: Small

Overnight parking: Allowed

Winter access: No

Special notes: This is a popular trailhead during peak times. If the small parking lot is full, do not park along the road—please find another place to recreate.

SECTION SNAPSHOT

Trail Atlas maps: C-2, C-3

Total distance: 8.7 miles (Additional 0.2-mile spur trail to Gooseberry Falls State Park Visitor Center Trailhead)

Elevation change: Despite a couple of short but challenging climbs, this section is predominantly gentle, especially where it follows the Gooseberry River.

SHT campsites: Five

Hazards and concerns: This section is rocky in places with poor footing along the banks of the Gooseberry River. There are many state park trail intersections.

Synopsis: This section features stately pine trees near Wolf Rock, several big views of Lake Superior, and a pleasant stretch along the bank of the Gooseberry River.

Pro tip: A reroute in this area is on the horizon, so as always, check for updates before hitting the Trail.

SPUR TRAILS

- **Crow Creek Valley Overlook.** This 0.1-mile spur trail offers an inland vista of the gorgeous Crow Creek Valley.
- **Gooseberry Falls State Park Trails.** Part of this section intersects with several trails within the extensive Gooseberry Falls State Park trail network. Countless loops can be created by studying a state park map.

CAMPSITES

▲ **Crow Valley Campsite**
Size: Medium
Water source: A small creek running through the campsite, unreliable in late season or when especially dry
This campsite is extremely busy due to the long distance between this site and Silver Creek Campsite to the south.
14.1, 8.4 ⊕ ⊕ 3.2, 4.1

▲ **West Gooseberry River Campsite**
Size: Medium
Water source: Gooseberry River
Campsite sits on a knoll above the river.
11.6, 3.2 ⊕ ⊕ 0.9, 1.0

▲ **East Gooseberry River Campsite**
Size: Small
Water source: Gooseberry River
Campsite is very small but offers good access to the river.
4.1, 0.9 ⊕ ⊕ 0.1, 0.9

▲ **Middle Gooseberry River Campsite**
Size: Small
Water source: Gooseberry River
Campsite is very small but offers good access to the river.
1.0, 0.1 ⊕ ⊕ 0.8, 7.0

▲ **Gooseberry River Campsite**

Size: Large

Water source: Gooseberry River

Campsite is on a short spur above the river. This site is the best option for group use in this area.

0.9, 0.8 ⊖ ⊕ 6.2, 10.1

MILEAGE	Northbound	Southbound
West Castle Danger Road Trailhead	**0.0**	**8.9**
Wolf Rock Vista	0.3	8.6
Spur to Crow Creek Valley Overlook	*1.1*	*7.8*
Crow Valley Campsite	1.2	7.7
Mike's Rock Vista	2.8	6.1
Nestor Grade crossing	3.8	5.1
West Gooseberry Campsite	4.4	4.5
East Gooseberry Campsite	5.3	3.5
Middle Gooseberry Campsite	5.4	3.6
Snowmobile trail crossing	5.7	3.3
Gooseberry Campsite	6.2	2.7
State park boundary marker	6.4	2.5
Day-use shelter	6.7	2.2
Fifth Falls bridge	7.7	1.2
Spur to Gooseberry Falls State Park Visitor Center Trailhead	*8.7*	*0.2*
Gooseberry Falls State Park Visitor Center Trailhead	**8.9**	**0.0**

Gooseberry Falls State Park Visitor Center Trailhead to Split Rock River Wayside Trailhead

Directions and GPS Waypoints: At MN-61 milepost 38.9, turn south, go 0.2 miles to Visitor Center parking lot. GPS: 47.138729, -91.469345

Facilities: Toilet, potable water, visitor center, state park fee campsites

Size: Large

Overnight parking: No. Overnight parking is allowed within Gooseberry Falls State Park. Permit required for overnight parking. Check in with state park staff. The overnight parking area adds nearly a mile on state park trails to reach the visitor center.

Winter access: Yes

Special notes: Gooseberry Falls State Park is one of the most visited state parks in Minnesota. Expect to share the Trail with other visitors throughout the year.

Trail Atlas maps: C-3, C-4

Total distance: 6.1 miles (Additional 0.2-mile spur trail from Gooseberry Falls State Park Visitor Center Trailhead; additional 0.5-mile spur trail to Split Rock River Wayside Trailhead)

Elevation change: This section is one of the flattest as it follows the Gitchi-Gami State Trail and Blueberry Hill Road for most of its miles. One climb along Breadloaf Ridge is the only noteworthy elevation change.

SHT campsites: One

Hazards and concerns: Watch for bike traffic on the Gitchi-Gami State Trail. Use caution when crossing Highway 61 and while navigating the roadwalk along Blueberry Hill Road. Be aware of drop-offs on Breadloaf Ridge.

Synopsis: Beginning gently, Trail follows a detour on the paved Gitchi-Gami State Trail to the dirt Blueberry Hill Road, then enters the woods and ascends to spectacular views from Breadloaf Ridge.

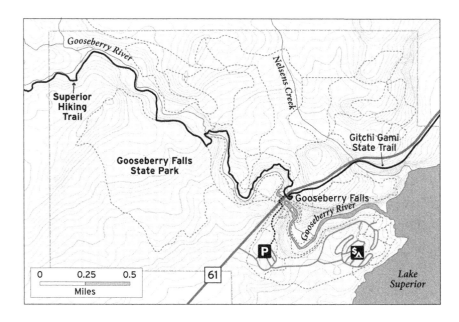

Pro tip: A new route in this area is on the horizon, so as always, check for updates before hitting the Trail.

SPUR TRAIL

▮ **Gooseberry Falls State Park Trails.** Part of this section intersects with several trails within the extensive Gooseberry Falls State Park trail network. Countless loops can be created by studying a state park map.

CAMPSITE

▲ **Blueberry Hill Campsite**
Size: Medium
Water source: Unreliable stream just north of the campsite
The sunny and spacious campsite makes a great place to take a break before or after the Blueberry Hill Road roadwalk.
7.0, 6.2 ⬅ ➔ 3.9, 4.2

MILEAGE	Northbound	Southbound
Gooseberry Falls State Park Visitor Center	**0.0**	**6.8**
Spur from Gooseberry Falls State Park Visitor Center Trailhead	0.2	6.6
Gitchi-Gami State Trail south end	0.2	6.6
Gitchi-Gami State Trail north end	2.6	4.2
Highway 61 crossing	2.6	4.2
Blueberry Hill roadwalk south end	2.6	4.2
Blueberry Hill Road roadwalk north end	3.8	3.0
Blueberry Hill Campsite	3.9	2.9
Breadloaf Ridge	4.7	2.1
State park boundary marker	5.3	1.5
Spur to Split Rock River Wayside Trailhead	6.3	0.5
Split Rock River Wayside Trailhead	**6.8**	**0.0**

The Gooseberry Gap: A Cautionary Tale

The Gooseberry Gap is truly a cautionary tale to all trail users—follow the rules of the Trail. It is paramount that Trail users understand the delicate land ownership behind the Superior Hiking Trail. Here are three lessons to take to heart:

Lesson one, the Superior Hiking Trail Association does not own the 300-mile Trail corridor. The Trail relies on over 240 private and public landowners to grant us access easements for the trail corridor. Each SHT user and their interaction with these landowners reflects on us as a whole trail community.

Lesson two, the Superior Hiking Trail Association must remain in good standing with each public and private landowner along the Trail in order to keep the Trail intact. That means all SHT users must follow the rules of the Trail and practice Leave No Trace principles.

Lesson three, the Superior Hiking Trail Association's access agreement with private or public landowners could be revoked, forcing time-consuming, costly reroutes—some that could negatively impact the beauty, safety, and charm of what we now know the SHT to be today.

In 2015, the Superior Hiking Trail Association lost access to a critical parcel of private property that forced the footpath to temporarily reroute the Superior Hiking Trail on less than desirable roadwalk and the paved multi-use Gitchi-Gami State Trail that runs along Highway 61. The parcel, between Gooseberry Falls State Park and Split Rock River Wayside, was lost because of user error, and it has been a costly one to the Superior Hiking Trail Association.

Since that time, the SHTA has been diligently working to identify a new route that is environmentally sustainable, in accordance with land managers' rules and regulations, and financially feasible to build and maintain. The diminished user experience and safety has had a big impact on this section of the Superior Hiking Trail. Since the "gap" was created, the SHTA has been looking for solutions to fill it.

After careful evaluation by both trail design experts and an environmental consultant, an alternate route has emerged, pushing the route of the SHT farther west toward Skunk Creek. This was the most comprehensive alignment study completed on behalf of the SHTA to date, to ensure the Trail is a sustainable, enjoyable, and cost-effective route on public land.

The SHTA made the mistake of optimistically proclaiming that the new route in this area would open in 2017, and we've learned our lesson. However, we will say this: it's likely that the new route will be opening in the coming years. ⋀⋀

Split Rock River Wayside Trailhead to Lax Lake Road Trailhead

Directions and GPS Waypoints: At MN-61 milepost 43.5 on north side of highway. GPS: 47.265963, -91.309545

Facilities: Kiosk

Size: Large

Overnight parking: No. Overnight parking is allowed within Split Rock Lighthouse State Park near the fee campground parking area. Permit required. Check in with state park staff. The overnight parking area inside the park adds 1.5 miles on state park trails to reach the SHT.

Winter access: Yes

Special notes: Among the most popular trailheads to access the Superior Hiking Trail and the Split Rock River Loop, expect to encounter other users throughout much of the year, and have a backup plan to recreate elsewhere if the parking area is full. An additional parking option is at the Cove Point Trailhead (At MN-61 milepost 50.2, turn south on Cove Point Lodge Rd. Continue 0.1 miles to parking lot on right. GPS: 47.248200, -91.313058) located at Cove Point Lodge accessible via a spur trail.

SECTION SNAPSHOT

Trail Atlas maps: C-4, C-5

Total distance: 13.2 miles (Additional 0.5-mile spur trail from Split Rock River Wayside Trailhead)

Elevation change: Dramatic. There is significant climbing and descending in this section.

SHT campsites: Seven

Hazards and concerns: Poor condition of tread, particularly along Split Rock River Loop. A natural, unbridged crossing of the Split Rock River. Steep, rocky terrain.

Synopsis: This section follows the Split Rock River for several miles before climbing to a ridge with views of Lake Superior and Split Rock Lighthouse. Several other overlooks on ridges and rock outcroppings provide lake and inland views.

Pro tip: To avoid the natural crossing of the Split Rock River, a Highway 61 underpass near the wayside leads to the Gitchi-Gami State Trail. Follow this paved trail to another SHT spur trail which accesses the north side of the Split Rock River Loop.

SPUR TRAILS

- **Split Rock River Wayside Trailhead.** The 0.5-mile spur trail leads to the Superior Hiking Trail near Strand Creek Waterfall.

- **Split Rock River Wayside Northern Access.** A 0.7-mile spur trail leads under Highway 61, across the Split Rock River on the paved Gitchi-Gami State Trail, then crosses Highway 61 and ascends to the Superior Hiking Trail.

- **Split Rock Lighthouse State Park Access.** A spur trail follows state park trails and leads either 1.5 miles into Split Rock Lighthouse State Park and its overnight parking lot, or 2.1 miles to the Split Rock River Wayside. This intersection with state park trails means that countless loops can be created by studying a state park map.

- **Cove Point Loop.** Compared to the Split Rock River Loop, the 5.5-mile Cove Point Loop is much less-traveled, yet features great views and no challenging river crossing. This lollipop-style loop makes for a great day trip. It also offers another entry or exit point for those travelling in between the Split Rock River Wayside and Lax Lake Road trailheads.

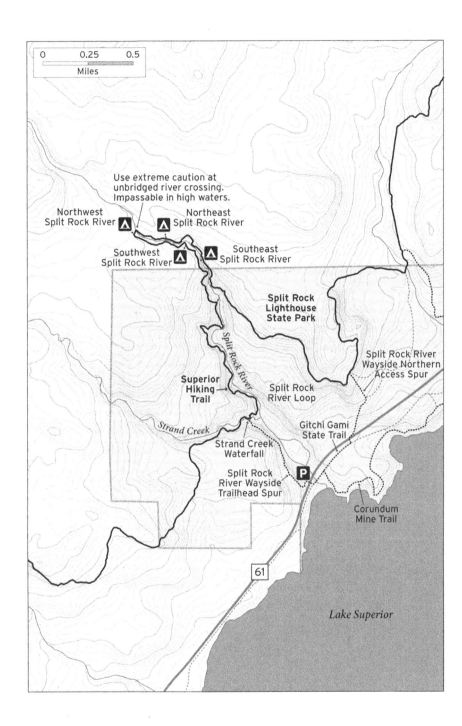

Use extreme caution at unbridged river crossing. Impassable in high waters.

Northwest Split Rock River

Northeast Split Rock River

Southwest Split Rock River

Southeast Split Rock River

Split Rock Lighthouse State Park

Split Rock River Wayside Northern Access Spur

Superior Hiking Trail

Split Rock River

Split Rock River Loop

Strand Creek

Strand Creek Waterfall

Gitchi Gami State Trail

Split Rock River Wayside Trailhead Spur

Corundum Mine Trail

61

Lake Superior

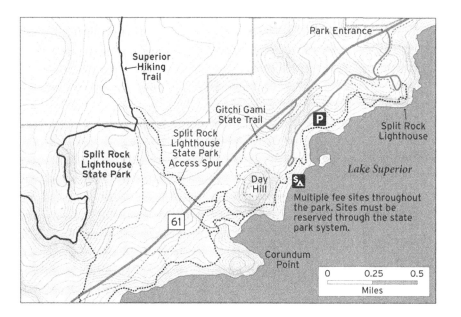

CAMPSITES

▲ **Southwest Split Rock River Campsite**

Size: Medium

Water source: Split Rock River

Campsite is often heavily used during peak periods.

10.1, 3.9 ⊙ ⊙ 0.3, 0.5

▲ **Northwest Split Rock River Campsite**

Size: Medium

Water source: Split Rock River

Campsite is near the river crossing.

4.2, 0.3 ⊙ ⊙ 0.2, 0.5

▲ **Northeast Split Rock River Campsite**

Size: Large

Water source: Split Rock River

Campsite is the best option for groups in this area.

0.5, 0.2 ⊙ ⊙ 0.3, 4.9

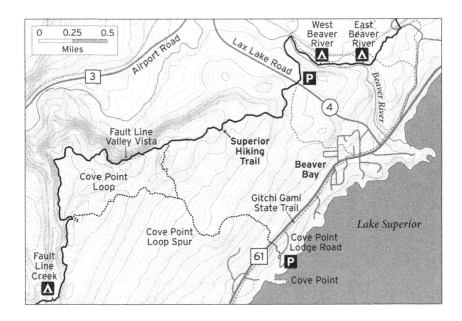

▲ **Southeast Split Rock River Campsite**

Size: Small

Water source: Split Rock River

Campsite is located close to the water but cannot accommodate many users.

0.5, 0.3 ⊙ ⊙ 4.6, 6.3

▲ **Chapins Ridge Campsite**

Size: Medium

Water source: A pond 0.2 miles north is the closest option. Please use extreme caution if you choose to have a fire; carry enough water to thoroughly douse any embers.

Campsite is set among large pines on a high ridge.

4.9, 4.6 ⊙ ⊙ 1.7, 3.1

▲ **Beaver Pond Campsite**

Size: Medium

Water source: A stagnant beaver pond

Lower tent pads may be unappealing in wet conditions.

6.3, 1.7 ⊙ ⊙ 1.4, 5.8

▲ **Fault Line Creek Campsite**

Size: Medium

Water source: A small beaver pond or Black Sand Creek

Campsite is adjacent to a mountain bike trail.

3.1, 1.4 ⊙ ⊙ 4.4, 4.7

MILEAGE	Northbound	Southbound
Split Rock River Wayside Trailhead	**0.0**	**14.2**
Spur to Split Rock River Wayside Trailhead	*0.5*	*13.7*
Strand Creek bridge	0.5	13.7
Register, view of waterfall	0.5	13.7
Split rocks	1.9	12.3
Southwest Split Rock River Campsite	2.0	12.2
Former bridge site	2.1	12.1
Northwest Split Rock River Campsite	2.3	11.9
Former bridge site	2.3	11.9
Northeast Split Rock River Campsite	2.5	11.7
Southeast Split Rock River Campsite	2.8	11.4
State park boundary marker	2.9	11.3
Day-use shelter	4.0	10.2
Northern spur to Split Rock River Wayside Trailhead	*4.1*	*10.1*
Vistas	4.5	9.7
Split Rock Creek bridge	5.2	9.0
Spur to Split Rock Lighthouse State Park or Split Rock River Wayside Trailhead	*5.3*	*8.9*
Merrill Grade Historic Logging Railroad	5.9	8.3
Chapins Ridge Campsite	7.4	6.8
ATV trail crossing	7.6	6.6
Christmas Tree Ridge	8.1	6.1
Beaver Pond Campsite	9.1	5.1
Vista with bench	9.6	4.6
Fault Line Creek Campsite	10.5	3.7
Cove Point Loop spur, west junction	*11.2*	*3.0*
Faultline Valley Vista	12.5	1.7
Cove Point Loop spur, east junction	*12.8*	*1.4*
Lax Lake Road crossing	14.2	0.0
Lake Lake Road Trailhead	**14.2**	**0.0**

Ongoing Renewal of the Split Rock River Loop

The Split Rock River Loop has long been a tourist destination on the North Shore. Increased traffic, particularly during wet conditions, has worsened the condition of the loop immeasurably. The Trail was placed in an optimal place for scenic quality, but not the ideal location for long-term sustainability. The steep edge of the river bluff has been continually eroding, playing a role in the compromised tread of the SHT here.

To further complicate the loop, its failing bridge was removed for safety reasons in 2016. This was the fourth bridge removed from the site in 25 years, though others were removed by high water and ice. Despite extensive research, no feasible solution for replacing the bridge has yet been found. The location is particularly challenging: with no road access nearer than Highway 61, supplies would require several dozen helicopter trips, a skilled crew willing to camp onsite, and a massive investment of resources.

In 2020, the Superior Hiking Trail Association decided to pause the project for the foreseeable future. While there may be a bridge here again someday, the SHTA refocused on other priorities—including some of the major erosion impacting the Trail along the Split Rock River.

The Split Rock River Loop can still be enjoyed most of the year. Frequent visitors enjoy out-and-back hikes just as much as a loop, and those who feel comfortable and confident in doing so have forded the Split Rock River. For trail users looking to bypass a ford, two spur trails leading from the main SHT to the Gitchi-Gami State Trail bridge near the mouth of the Split Rock River can be connected to avoid the area.

For goal-oriented hikers and runners, the SHTA does not differentiate between those who ford the river at the former bridge site and those who bypass it via the Gitchi-Gami State Trail. ⋀⋀

▍Lax Lake Road Trailhead to Penn Boulevard Trailhead

Directions and GPS Waypoints: At MN-61 milepost 51.1, turn north on Lax Lake Rd., go 0.8 miles to parking lot on right. GPS: 47.265963, -91.309545

Facilities: None

Size: Small

Overnight parking: Allowed

Winter access: Yes

Special notes: Trailhead is largely on private land; please use extra care to leave it better than you found it. Expect to encounter other users throughout much of the year, and have a backup plan to recreate elsewhere if the parking area is full.

SECTION SNAPSHOT

Trail Atlas maps: C-5, C-6

Total distance: 4.3 miles

Elevation change: A mostly-flat walk along the Beaver River leads to more noteworthy elevation change as the Trail traverses hills above Silver Bay.

SHT campsites: Two

Hazards and concerns: Use caution on the multi-use trail between Lax Lake Road and the Beaver River, and be aware of rocky, rooty terrain.

Synopsis: After hugging the gorgeous Beaver River, Trail climbs to expansive views of Lake Superior and Silver Bay.

CAMPSITES

▲ **West Beaver River Campsite**

Size: Small

Water source: Beaver River

Campsite is extremely heavily-used during peak periods.

5.8, 4.4 ⊖ ⊕ 0.3, 5.6

▲ **East Beaver River Campsite**

Size: Small

Water source: Beaver River

Campsite features nearby rocks with a view of the river. Campsite is extremely heavily-used during peak periods.

4.7, 0.3 ⊖ ⊕ 5.3, 6.5

MILEAGE	Northbound	Southbound
Lax Lake Road Trailhead	**0.0**	**4.3**
Beaver River bridge	0.3	4.0
West Beaver River Campsite	0.7	3.6
East Beaver River Campsite	1.0	3.3
Betzler Road crossing	1.1	3.2
Junction with Gitchi-Gami State Trail through underpass	1.5	2.8
Glacial erratic	1.6	2.7
ATV trail crossing	1.7	2.6
Golf Course Road, service road crossing	2.0	2.3
Silver Bay Vista	2.9	1.4
Penn Boulevard crossing	4.3	0.0
ATV trail crossing, spur to Penn Boulevard Trailhead	*4.3*	*0.0*
Penn Boulevard Trailhead	**4.3**	**0.0**

▌ Penn Boulevard Trailhead to Minnesota Highway 1 Trailhead

Directions and GPS Waypoints: At MN-61 milepost 54.3, turn northwest on Outer Drive, go 1.5 miles to Penn Blvd. Continue straight 0.5 miles on Penn Blvd. to parking lot on right. GPS: 47.291886, -91.298757

Facilities: None

Size: Large

Overnight parking: Allowed

Winter access: Yes

Special notes: Although this is among the largest SHT trailheads, it may be overcrowded during peak times, particularly on weekends in autumn. Expect to encounter other users throughout much of the year, and have a backup plan to recreate elsewhere if the parking area is full. An additional parking option is available at Bay Area Historical Society Trailhead (At MN-61 milepost 54.3, turn northwest on Outer Drive, go 0.5 miles to Bay Area Historical Society parking lot on right. GPS: 47.294977, -91.268692).

SECTION SNAPSHOT

Trail Atlas maps: C-6, C-7

Total distance: 10.7 miles

Elevation change: This section is frequently cited as among the hardest of the Superior Hiking Trail, in large part due to the extensive elevation change.

SHT campsites: Five

Hazards and concerns: Rocky and rooty tread, dramatic cliffs, erosion, state park trail network.

Synopsis: Climbing steadily from the trailhead, the SHT gains and loses elevation en route to vistas of Silver Bay and Bean and Bear Lakes. The Trail winds through the backcountry of Tettegouche State Park, passing Round Mountain and ascending Mount Trudee. Joining the state park trail network, the SHT passes several spur trails to overlooks and crosses the bridge over the Baptism River.

Pro tip: Use of this section drops off dramatically outside of the Bean and Bear Lakes Loop.

SPUR TRAILS

- **Bean and Bear Lakes Loop Spur.** This 1.2-mile spur trail leads 0.4 miles to Elam's Knob, a small overlook. Just 0.2 miles further, the spur trail encounters the Bay Area Historical Society spur trail (see below). Continuing northeast, in 0.6 miles the spur trail comes to the junction with the main SHT near the Bear Lake Overlook.

- **Bay Area Historical Society.** This spur trail, accessible from the middle of the Bean and Bear Lakes Loop Spur, leads 2.2 miles into downtown Silver Bay. Check a map to see how it can be enjoyed as its own lollipop-loop, or used as an alternate entry or exit point when accessing the vistas near Bean and Bear Lakes.

- **Round Mountain Mini-Loop.** A 0.3-mile roundtrip small loop summits Round Mountain and circles its top.

- **Hawk Hill.** An incredible vista of Mount Trudee is only 0.1 miles off the Superior Hiking Trail.

- **Raven Rock.** A vista located 0.1 miles off the Trail offers a compelling alternative for southbound trail users not wanting to travel all the way to Mount Trudee.

- **Red Pine Overlook.** A beautiful biome exists on this knob 0.1 miles off the Superior Hiking Trail.

- **Tettegouche State Park Trailhead.** A 0.3-mile state park trail leads to parking within Tettegouche State Park. State park permit required to drive or park here. Toilets available nearby as well as fee campsites.

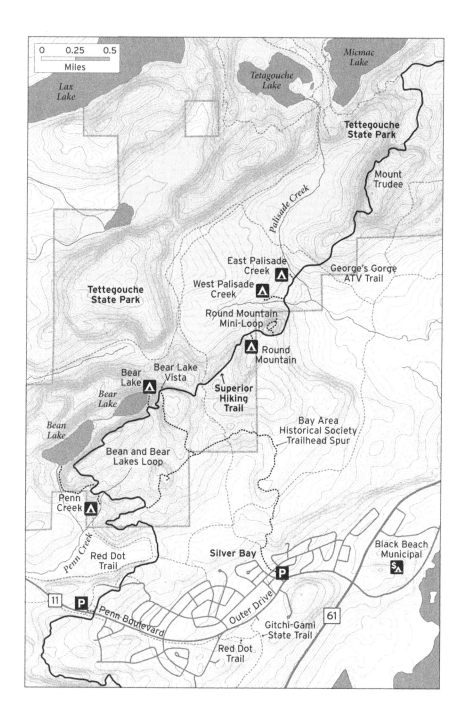

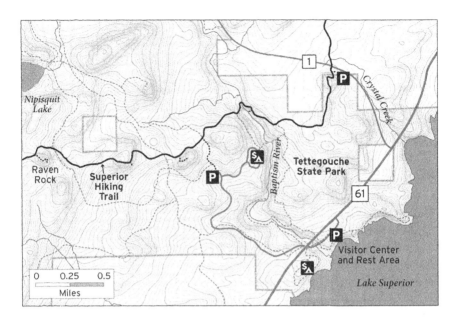

SPUR TRAILS, continued

▪ **Tettegouche State Park trails.** Part of this section intersects with several trails within the extensive Tettegouche State Park trail network. Countless loops can be created by studying a state park map.

▲ **Penn Creek Campsite**
Size: Large
Water source: Penn Creek, unreliable during dry periods. Creek has a hidden waterfall when flowing.
Campsite is located on a 0.1-mile spur trail and is the best option for group use in this area. Campsite has a picnic table and two latrines.
5.6, 5.3 ⊖ ⊝ 1.2, 2.4

▲ **Bear Lake Campsite**
Size: Small
Water source: Bear Lake
Hammock issues reported here.
Campsite is located on a 0.1-mile spur trail. It has a one-night limit due to being within Tettegouche State Park boundaries. Campsite has extremely poor tent pads, yet is the most heavily-used campsite on the Superior Hiking Trail. Make plans to camp elsewhere.
6.5, 1.2 ⊖ ⊝ 1.2, 1.7

▲ **Round Mountain Campsite**
Size: Medium
Water source: Beaver pond, reliable but often stagnant
Campsite offers a good alternative for those wanting to avoid crowds at Bear Lake Campsite. Nearby access to Round Mountain Mini-Loop.
2.4, 1.2 ⊖ ⊝ 0.5, 0.6

▲ **West Palisade Creek Campsite**
Size: Medium
Water source: West Palisade Creek, a small and somewhat reliable creek. If dry, the east branch of the creek is nearby.
Campsite is on a 0.1-mile spur trail in the shadow of Round Mountain. There are views of the surrounding landscape during leaf-off season.
1.7, 0.5 ⊖ ⊝ 0.1, 8.1

▲ **East Palisade Creek Campsite**
Size: Large
Water source: East Palisade Creek, a small but reliable creek
Large campsite is the best option for group use in this area.
0.6, 0.1 ⊖ ⊝ 8.0, 8.0

MILEAGE	Northbound	Southbound
Penn Boulevard Trailhead	**0.0**	**10.7**
Spur from Penn Boulevard Trailhead	0.0	10.7
Service road crossing	0.3	10.4
Power line corridor	0.4	10.3
ATV trail crossing	0.7	10.0
Bean and Bear Lakes Loop spur, west junction	1.6	9.1
Spur to Penn Creek Campsite	*2.0*	*8.7*
Spur to Bear Lake Campsite	*3.2*	*7.5*
Register, *Bean and Bear Lakes Loop spur,* *east junction*	*3.5*	*7.2*
George's Gorge ATV trail crossing	3.8	6.9
Round Mountain Campsite	4.4	6.3
Spur to Round Mountain mini-loop	*4.6*	*6.1*
West Palisade Campsite	4.9	5.8
East Palisade Campsite	5.0	5.7
George's Gorge ATV trail crossing	5.3	5.4
Mount Trudee	6.5	4.2
Spur to Hawk Hill	*7.0*	*3.7*
Spur to Raven Rock	*7.6*	*3.1*
The Drainpipe	8.5	2.2
Spur to Red Pine Overlook	*9.1*	*1.6*
Spur to Tettegouche State Park Trailhead	*9.3*	*1.4*
State park trail to campground	9.5	1.2
Baptism River swinging bridge	9.6	1.1
State park trail to High Falls Lower Vista	9.7	1.0
State park trail to Two Step Falls	9.9	0.8
Spur to Minnesota Highway 1 Trailhead	*10.7*	*0.0*
Minnesota Highway 1 Trailhead	**10.7**	**0.0**

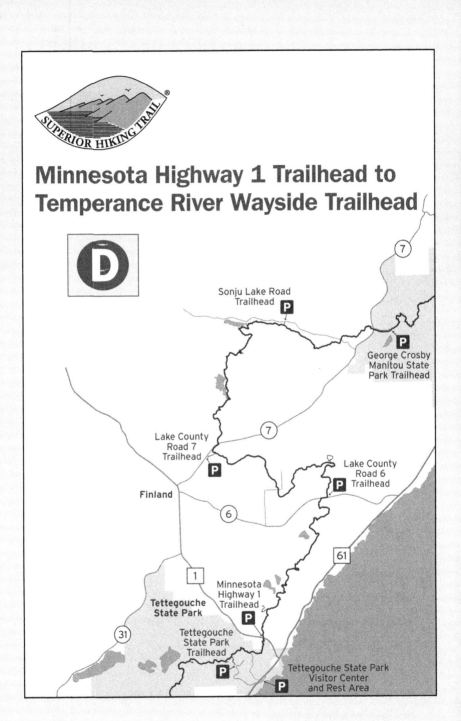

Minnesota Highway 1 Trailhead to Temperance River Wayside Trailhead

D

Sonju Lake Road Trailhead **P**

⑦

P George Crosby Manitou State Park Trailhead

Lake County Road 7 Trailhead **P**

⑦

Lake County Road 6 Trailhead **P**

Finland

⑥

61

1

Minnesota Highway 1 Trailhead **P**

Tettegouche State Park

㉛

Tettegouche State Park Trailhead **P**

Tettegouche State Park Visitor Center and Rest Area **P**

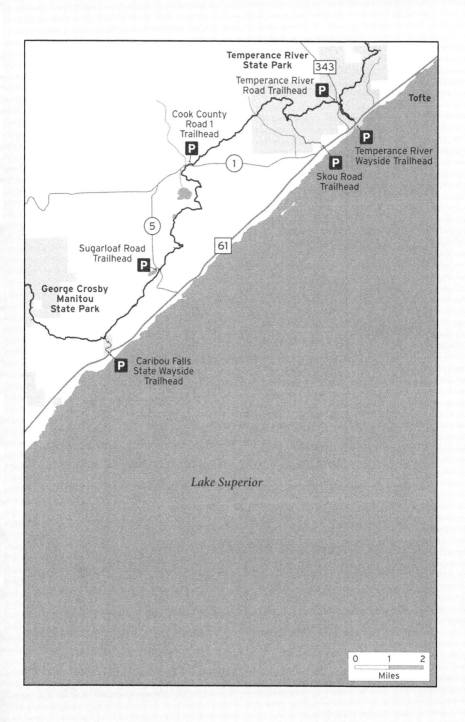

Minnesota Highway 1 Trailhead to Temperance River Wayside Trailhead

▌ Overview

From **Minnesota Highway 1 Trailhead,** the Superior Hiking Trail heads north toward a spur trail to Fantasia Overlook. The Trail winds along rock outcroppings with views of Lake Superior. Near Wolf Ridge Environmental Learning Center, the Trail comes to a view of Wolf Lake and distant education buildings. The forest in this area was impacted by a dramatic 2009 ice storm: bent trees from here into Cook County are reminders of that event. Sawmill Dome provides one of the most-beloved panoramas of the entire Trail with a view of the nearby Section 13 cliffs. The descent to County Road 6 is exceptionally rugged.

The **Lake County Road 6 Trailhead** leads to the spectacular Section 13 cliffs, named by the climbers who often utilize its rock faces. A wide, sturdy boardwalk across Sawmill Creek Pond provides a safe crossing over a major beaver dam. The Trail passes an impressive glacial erratic, dropped in place when the glaciers receded thousands of years ago. A low, wet area around Leskinen Creek has an impressive amount of mud before the Trail climbs to a wooded ridgeline and eventually over the East Branch of the Baptism River. A spur trail connects to the Lake County Road 7 Trailhead.

From the **Lake County Road 7 Trailhead**, a spur trail connects to the main Superior Hiking Trail before crossing Lake County Road 7 and continuing north. After crossing Egge Creek on a small bridge, the Trail passes Egge Lake and travels through dense forest to Sonju Lake. A boardwalk leads to Lilly's Island—a small collection of trees and rocks that, depending on the lake level, look more or less like an island. The Trail travels over rooty, rocky but fairly level terrain before crossing the East Branch of the Baptism River.

Sonju Lake Road Trailhead is connected to the Superior Hiking Trail by a short spur trail. The Trail here heads generally east on its way to George Crosby Manitou State Park. Many cedar roots make for challenging footing, but the Trail is fairly level as it follows the East Branch of the Baptism River and crosses Blesener Creek. When the Trail crosses Lake County Road 7 again, a roadwalk on the narrow, dirt Benson Lake Road brings the Trail into the state park.

From **George Crosby Manitou State Park Trailhead,** the Superior Hiking Trail is easy to miss among other park trails in the vicinity. The route through the park is exceptionally challenging; the Trail here is a tangle of roots and rocks with magnificent elevation change. The Superior Hiking Trail drops down into the stunning Manitou River Valley and crosses the river on a bridge. One of the most dramatic ascents of the entire Trail follows, leading steeply to Horseshoe Ridge with views of Lake Superior and the Manitou River Valley. The Trail descends toward Caribou River, crossing its gorge on an impressive bridge. A spur trail leads east to Caribou Falls.

At **Caribou Falls State Wayside Trailhead,** a spur trail heads to a stairway which leads to the base of Caribou Falls. The spur trail continues uphill to the main Superior Hiking Trail. The Trail continues from the Caribou River where forest succession is on display as bent birch die off. The majority of the land in this section is privately owned; as always, treat the land with respect and stay on the Trail. The southernmost power line crossing marks the boundary between Lake and Cook Counties. A unique covered bridge spans Crystal Creek, and near the adjacent campsite is an abandoned mine. A pine plantation carpets the flat, fairly level way to Sugarloaf Road.

Sugarloaf Road Trailhead starts one of the gentler sections of the Superior Hiking Trail. The Trail crosses Sugarloaf Creek and the ever-shrinking Sugarloaf Pond (visible from the adjacent campsite). Ruffy Lake, formerly known as Alfred's Pond, is a perfect place to sit on a bench and appreciate the unique plants and animals of the area. After a steep ascent and descent, the Trail comes to an A-frame bridge over Dyer's Creek and follows Two Island River, crossing abandoned railroad tracks and Cook County Road 1 before reaching the next trailhead.

From **Cook County Road 1 Trailhead,** the Superior Hiking Trail slowly rises through deep woods to a couple openings with Lake Superior views, including Tower Overlook. A descent to unbridged Fredenberg Creek is followed by Boney's Meadow before arriving at the tumbling Cross River. The Trail follows the river, at times over many rocks, to a large bridge. Just north of the bridge is a spur trail downhill to Skou Road Trailhead.

From **Skou Road Trailhead,** a long spur trail ascends ski and hiking trails to reach the main Superior Hiking Trail. The route toward Temperance River State Park meanders through a pine forest until the final, dramatic descent to Temperance River Road. The Superior Hiking Trail follows the scenic Temperance River downstream to a short spur trail to Highway 61 and the Temperance River Wayside Trailhead. ⋀⋀

Minnesota Highway 1 Trailhead to Lake County Road 6 Trailhead

Directions and GPS Waypoints: At MN-61 milepost 59.3, turn north on MN-1, go 0.8 miles to parking lot on left. GPS: 47.354927, -91.195618

Facilities: None

Size: Small

Overnight parking: Allowed

Winter access: No

Special notes: This small parking lot may be full during peak times. An alternative parking lot is available within Tettegouche State Park with a state park permit.

SECTION SNAPSHOT

Trail Atlas maps: D-1, D-2

Total distance: 7.0 miles

Elevation change: There is significant elevation change in this area with some level stretches interspersed.

SHT campsites: Two

Hazards and concerns: There are rock ledges and steep terrain with rocks and roots. Use caution when crossing Highway 1.

Synopsis: Highlights include many views from rock outcroppings and the deep Finland forest. Fantasia Overlook and Sawmill Dome are noteworthy vistas.

Pro tip: Wolf Ridge Environmental Learning Center is a gracious landowner that allows the Superior Hiking Trail across its unique property. Please respect private property here by staying on the Trail and avoiding Wolf Ridge ELC's private infrastructure.

▪ **Fantasia Overlook.** A 0.4-mile spur trail leads to a gorgeous inland overlook.

▪ **Picnic Rock.** It's just 0.1 miles to this overlook—a great addition to any trip on this section.

CAMPSITES

▲ **West Kennedy Creek Campsite**
Size: Medium
Water source: Kennedy Creek, unreliable in dry conditions
Campsite is located on private property. Please follow the posted campsite rules and do not trespass outside the bounds of the campsite.
8.1, 8.0 ⊖ ⊕ 0.0, 6.1

▲ **East Kennedy Creek Campsite**
Size: Medium
Water source: Kennedy Creek, unreliable in dry conditions
Campsite is located on private property. Please follow the posted campsite rules and do not trespass outside the bounds of the campsite.
8.0, 0.0 ⊖ ⊕ 6.1, 9.8

MILEAGE	Northbound	Southbound
Minnesota Highway 1 Trailhead	**0.0**	**7.0**
Spur from Minnesota Highway 1 Trailhead	*0.0*	*7.0*
Minnesota Highway 1 crossing, power line corridor	0.0	7.0
Crystal Creek bridge	0.1	6.9
Spur to Fantasia Overlook	*1.0*	*6.0*
Short ATV trail junction	1.3	5.7
West Kennedy Creek Campsite	2.3	4.7
East Kennedy Creek Campsite	2.3	4.7
Power line corridor	3.1	3.9
Lime Squeezer	3.9	3.1
Sawmill Dome Vista	5.5	1.5
Spur to Picnic Rock	*5.7*	*1.3*
Lake County Road 6 crossing, roadwalk west end	6.8	0.2
Lake County Road 6 roadwalk east end	7.0	0.0
Lake County Road 6 Trailhead	**7.0**	**0.0**

Lake County Road 6 Trailhead to Lake County Road 7 Trailhead

Directions and GPS Waypoints: At MN-61 milepost 65.3, turn west on Lake Co. Rd. 6, go 2.3 miles to parking lot on right. GPS: 47.411691, -91.154728

Facilities: None

Size: Medium

Overnight parking: Allowed

Winter access: Yes

Special notes: Trailhead is shared with rock climbers and backcountry skiers. Expect to encounter other users throughout much of the year, and have a backup plan to recreate elsewhere if the parking area is full.

SECTION SNAPSHOT

Trail Atlas map: D-2

Total distance: 7.2 miles (Additional 0.3-mile spur trail to Lake County Road 7 Trailhead)

Elevation change: There are several climbs on this stretch, most notably the climb to the Section 13 cliffs.

SHT campsites: Two

Hazards and concerns: Cliff edges, rocky terrain, and significant mud near Leskinen Creek

Synopsis: Trail climbs to inspiring views at the Section 13 cliffs, descends steeply to Sawmill Creek Pond, passes a large glacial erratic, and winds through a low, wet area before ascending a ridge and descending to the East Branch of the Baptism River.

Pro tip: The low-lying parts of this section are an opportunity to view unique plants and even spot signs of moose.

SPUR TRAIL

▪ **Section 13 Loop.** The loop, in the process of being rehabilitated as of this writing, will someday provide more vistas of the Section 13 area. Spur trail was infrequently maintained for many years in the aftermath of a dramatic ice storm.

CAMPSITES

▲ **Section 13 Campsite**
Size: Medium
Water source: None. Nearest source is 0.5 miles north at a small creek. Small campsite has an upper and lower portion. Unsuitable for large groups. This heavily-used site has a history of attracting animals; please take extra care to protect your food and pack out what you bring in to keep the site clean.
6.1, 6.1 ⊖ ⊖ 3.7, 8.3

▲ **Leskinen Creek Campsite**
Size: Medium
Water source: Small, shallow creek just north of the campsite Campsite is located in prime bear habitat; please take extra caution to protect your food and pack out what you bring in to keep the site clean.
9.8, 3.7 ⊖ ⊖ 4.6, 4.8

MILEAGE	Northbound	Southbound
Lake County Road 6 Trailhead	**0.0**	**7.5**
Sawmill Creek bridge	0.3	7.2
Short spur to vista	*1.2*	*6.3*
Section 13 Vista	1.4	6.1
Section 13 Campsite	1.4	6.1
Spur to Section 13 Loop	*1.8*	*5.7*
Sawmill Creek Pond boardwalk, register	2.9	4.6
Glacial erratic	3.8	3.7
Park Hill Road crossing	4.3	3.2
Leskinen Creek Campsite	5.1	2.4
Mickleson Road crossing	6.6	0.9
East Branch Baptism River bridge	7.1	0.4
Spur to Lake County Road 7 Trailhead	*7.2*	*0.3*
Lake County Road 7 Trailhead	**7.5**	**0.0**

Lake County Road 7 Trailhead to Sonju Lake Road Trailhead

BEGINNING TRAILHEAD

Directions and GPS Waypoints: At MN-61 milepost 59.3, turn north on MN-1, go 6.0 miles to Lake Co. Rd. 7 . Turn northeast, go 1.3 miles to parking lot on right. GPS: 47.429502, -91.228446

Facilities: Toilet, kiosk

Size: Large

Overnight parking: Allowed

Winter access: Yes

Special notes: This trailhead is shared with North Shore State Trail users.

SECTION SNAPSHOT

Trail Atlas maps: D-2, D-3

Total distance: 7.3 miles (Additional 0.3-mile spur trail from Lake County Road 7 Trailhead)

Elevation change: A rolling section of trail with no major climbs

SHT campsites: Four

Hazards and concerns: Multiple crossings of logging roads and the North Shore State Trail in the area

Synopsis: This section highlights the beauty of several streams and Egge and Sonju lakes. Though remote, and with lots of roots to navigate, this section has comparatively little elevation change, making it one of the easier sections of the SHT.

Pro tip: The lakes in this section are popular destinations, particularly on weekends.

SPUR TRAILS

- **Egge Creek.** A little-used and infrequently-maintained spur trail follows Egge Creek 100 feet to the North Shore State Trail. Spur trail can be used to create a loop with the NSST.

- **Lilly's Island.** No trip to Sonju Lake is complete without venturing out to Lilly's Island, just 130 feet off the main SHT. A trail register on the island invites reflection.

▪ **Sonju Lake Road Trailhead.** A 250-foot spur trail leads to Sonju Lake Road Trailhead.

CAMPSITES

▲ **South Egge Lake Campsite**
Size: Medium
Water source: Egge Lake, with better water access at nearby Egge Creek 0.2 miles south
Campsite offers easy access to Egge Lake.
8.3, 4.6 ⊛ ⊛ 0.2, 3.2

▲ **North Egge Lake Campsite**
Size: Medium
Water source: Egge Lake
Campsite offers easy access to Egge Lake with slightly less traffic at this site compared to its neighbor.
4.8, 0.2 ⊛ ⊛ 3.0, 3.3

▲ **South Sonju Lake Campsite**
Size: Large
Water source: Sonju Lake, with better water access from nearby Lilly's Island
Large campsite is the best option for group use on this section.
3.2, 3.0 ⊛ ⊛ 0.3, 2.1

▲ **North Sonju Lake Campsite**
Size: Medium
Water source: Sonju Lake. Can be challenging to get water at this site's lake access without stirring up mud.
Sloped campsite offers few usable tent pads.
3.3, 0.3 ⊛ ⊛ 1.8, 2.4

MILEAGE	Northbound	Southbound
Lake County Road 7 Trailhead	**0.0**	**7.6**
Spur from Lake County Road 7 Trailhead	*0.3*	*7.3*
Lake County Road 7 crossing, roadwalk west end	0.5	7.1
Lake County Road 7 roadwalk east end	0.7	6.9
North Shore State Trail crossing	0.9	6.7
North Shore State Trail crossing	1.3	6.3
Spur to North Shore State Trail	*2.6*	*5.0*
Egge Creek bridge	2.6	5.0
South Egge Lake Campsite	2.8	4.8
North Egge Lake Campsite	3.0	4.6
South Sonju Lake Campsite	6.0	1.6
Spur to Lilly's Island, register	*6.0*	*1.6*
North Sonju Lake Campsite	6.3	1.3
East Branch Baptism bridge	7.6	0.0
Spur to Sonju Lake Road Trailhead	*7.6*	*0.0*
Sonju Lake Road Trailhead	**7.6**	**0.0**

▎Sonju Lake Road Trailhead to George Crosby Manitou State Park Trailhead

Directions and GPS Waypoints: At MN-61 milepost 59.3, turn north on MN-1, go 6.0 miles to Lake Co. Rd. 7. Turn northeast, go 6.7 miles to Sonju Lake Rd. Slight turn west, go 2.4 miles to parking lot on left. GPS: 47.483322, -91.177956

Facilities: None

Size: Small

Overnight parking: Allowed

Winter access: No

Special notes: Sonju Lake Road is a narrow forest road with many curves and frequent logging truck traffic. Use extreme caution, especially when icy.

SECTION SNAPSHOT

Trail Atlas maps: D-3, D-4

Total distance: 4.0 miles

Elevation change: Minimal

SHT campsites: Three

Hazards and concerns: Many roots and rocks cover this section. Use caution on the Benson Lake Road roadwalk.

Synopsis: Highlighting the cedar habitat along the East Branch of the Baptism River, this section is a fairly flat forest walk with one overlook toward the north end.

Pro tip: For those who like to bike on gravel roads, this is a great section to self-shuttle between trailheads.

CAMPSITES

▲ **East Branch Baptism River Campsite**
  Size: Small
  Water source: East Branch Baptism River
  Small site with little privacy from the Trail has access to the river which, in season, swarms with dragonflies.
  2.1, 1.8 ⊖ ⊕ 0.6, 2.6

▲ **Blesener Creek Campsite**
Size: Small
Water source: East Branch Baptism River or Blesener Creek
Small campsite among cedars. Uniquely situated between two water bodies. Campsite is not far from the North Shore State Trail crossing and NSST infrastructure, including a shelter and an outhouse.
2.4, 0.6 ⊖ ⊕ 2.0, 7.0

▲ **Aspen Knob Campsite**
Size: Small
Water source: Small creek just north of campsite
Campsite is not far from rural roads and homesteads; some noise from these places should be expected.
2.6, 2.0 ⊖ ⊕ 5.0, 7.8

MILEAGE	Northbound	Southbound
Sonju Lake Road Trailhead	**0.0**	**4.0**
Spur from Sonju Lake Road Trailhead	*0.0*	*4.0*
East Branch Baptism River Campsite	0.5	3.5
Blesener Creek Campsite	1.1	2.9
North Shore State Trail crossing, nearby shelter	1.3	2.7
Sonju Lake Road crossing	2.3	1.7
Blesner Lake Road crossing	3.1	0.9
Aspen Knob Campsite	3.2	0.8
Vista	3.4	0.6
Lake County Road 7 crossing	3.5	0.5
Benson Lake Road roadwalk west end	3.5	0.5
Spur to water pump	*3.8*	*0.2*
Benson Lake Road roadwalk east end	4.0	0.0
George Crosby Manitou State Park Trailhead	**4.0**	**0.0**

George Crosby Manitou State Park Trailhead to Caribou Falls State Wayside Trailhead

BEGINNING TRAILHEAD

Directions and GPS Waypoints: At MN-61 milepost 59.3, turn north on MN-1, go 6.0 miles to Lake Co. Rd. 7. Turn northeast, go 7.8 miles to entrance of George Crosby Manitou State Park. Turn east, go 0.5 miles to parking lot on left. GPS: 47.478642, -91.112585

Facilities: Toilet, nearby water, kiosk, state park fee campsites

Size: Large

Overnight parking: Allowed

Winter access: Yes, at the entrance kiosk. The main parking lot is unplowed in the winter, but there is a plowed parking area about 0.3 miles west of the trailhead.

Special notes: State park permit required for day use and overnight parking.

SECTION SNAPSHOT

Trail Atlas maps: D-4, D-5

Total distance: 7.0 miles (Additional 0.7-mile spur trail to Caribou Falls State Wayside Trailhead)

Elevation change: Area is known for its steep elevation changes, often cited as one of the hardest sections. The most challenging parts of the section are on the southwestern side; the northeastern third of the section is significantly less challenging.

SHT campsites: Two

Hazards and concerns: Expect to encounter rugged terrain, steep drop-offs, and remoteness.

Synopsis: Trail wanders through George Crosby Manitou State Park on state park trails before crossing the rushing Manitou River and climbing steeply to Horseshoe Ridge. The Trail has many overlooks before it descends toward Caribou River.

Pro tip: Not only one of the hardest but also one of the longest shuttles of any section, there is no quick way to drive between this section's trailheads.

▮ **George Crosby Manitou State Park Trails.** Part of this section intersects with several trails within the extensive George Crosby Manitou State Park network. Countless loops can be created by studying a state park map.

▮ **Overlooked Overlook.** A 0.1-mile spur trail leads to a modest view, but efforts to reclaim the full, now-overgrown route to the real Overlooked Overlook are underway.

▮ **Caribou Falls State Wayside Trailhead.** A 0.7-mile spur trail leads downhill 0.2 miles to the base of Caribou Falls and an additional 0.5 miles to the trailhead.

CAMPSITES

Special note: The Superior Hiking Trail passes by a few backpack-in campsites managed by the state park. These campsites require reservations and payment in advance, unlike the campsites managed by the SHTA. There is unlikely to be any cell reception within the park, so plan accordingly.

▲ **Horseshoe Ridge Campsite**
Size: Medium
Water source: An unreliable stream near the campsite
Campsite is not suitable for large groups. Please consider reserving a campsite within George Crosby Manitou State Park.
7.0, 5.0 ⊛ ⊛ 2.8, 2.9

▲ **West Caribou River Campsite**
Size: Small
Water source: Caribou River
Small campsite sits on a rise above the river.
Campsite is not suitable for large groups. Please consider reserving a campsite within George Crosby Manitou State Park.
7.8, 2.8 ⊛ ⊛ 0.1, 1.5

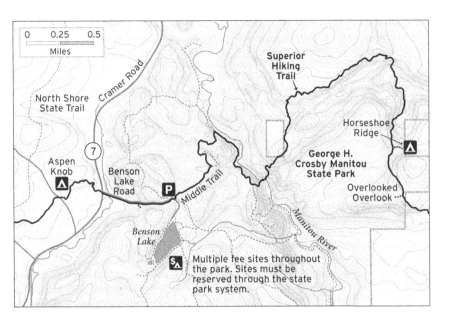

MILEAGE	Northbound	Southbound
George Crosby Manitou State Park Trailhead	**0.0**	**7.7**
Day-use shelter	0.7	7.0
State park campsite 3, fee and reservation required	1.0	6.7
State park campsite 4, fee and reservation required	1.1	6.6
State park bridge	1.2	6.5
Manitou River bridge	1.6	6.1
Manitou River Valley Vista	1.9	5.8
Horseshoe Ridge Vista	3.5	4.2
Horseshoe Ridge Campsite	4.1	3.6
Spur to Overlooked Overlook	*4.4*	*3.3*
Bob Silver Logging Road crossing (private road)	5.9	1.8
Pork Bay Trail sign	6.3	1.4
West Caribou River Campsite	6.9	0.8
Spur to Caribou Falls and Caribou Falls State Wayside Trailhead	*7.0*	*0.7*
Spur to Caribou Falls	*7.2*	*0.5*
Caribou Falls State Wayside Trailhead	***7.7***	***0.0***

Caribou Falls State Wayside Trailhead to Sugarloaf Road Trailhead

Directions and GPS Waypoints: At MN-61 milepost 70.5 on north side of highway. GPS: 47.464308, -91.030424

Facilities: Toilet

Size: Large

Overnight parking: No

Winter access: Unlikely

Special notes: Trailhead is near the border of Lake and Cook counties, located in a curve on Highway 61. Use caution!

SECTION SNAPSHOT

Trail Atlas map: D-5

Total distance: 2.9 miles (Additional 0.7-mile spur trail from Caribou Falls State Wayside Trailhead)

Elevation change: The majority of elevation change on this section is on the spur trail from Caribou Falls State Wayside Trailhead.

SHT campsites: Two

Hazards and concerns: Steep drop-offs near the Caribou River

Synopsis: Rolling section with views of Lake Superior through the trees. The Trail crosses Crystal Creek and heads through a pine plantation.

Pro tip: Spur trail to Crystal Creek Campsite is worth the extra steps, even for those not camping there.

SPUR TRAIL

■ **Caribou Falls State Wayside Trailhead.** A 0.7-mile spur trail leads uphill 0.5 miles to the base of Caribou Falls and an additional 0.2 miles to the Superior Hiking Trail.

CAMPSITES

▲ **East Caribou River Campsite**
Size: Large
Water source: Caribou River
Large campsite is the best option for group use in the area. Note that although this campsite is close to the trailhead, overnight parking is not allowed at Caribou Falls State Wayside Trailhead.
2.9, 0.1 ⊕ ⊕ 1.4, 3.6

▲ **Crystal Creek Campsite**
Size: Medium
Water source: Crystal Creek
Campsite is on a 0.2-mile spur trail and located on private property. Please follow the posted campsite rules and do not trespass outside the bounds of the campsite. Campsite is adjacent to an old mine.
1.5, 1.4 ⊕ ⊕ 2.6, 6.0

MILEAGE	Northbound	Southbound
Caribou Falls State Wayside Trailhead	**0.0**	**3.6**
Spur to Caribou Falls	0.5	3.1
Spur from Caribou Falls and Caribou Falls Wayside Trailhead	0.7	2.9
Register	0.7	2.9
East Caribou River Campsite	0.7	2.9
Power line corridor, Lake/Cook County border	1.5	2.1
Spur to Crystal Creek Campsite	2.1	1.5
Crystal Creek covered bridge	2.2	1.4
Power line corridor	2.8	0.8
High Ridge Drive crossing (private road)	3.5	0.1
Sugarloaf Road Trailhead	**3.6**	**1.0**

▌ Sugarloaf Road Trailhead to Cook County Road 1 Trailhead

Directions and GPS Waypoints: At MN-61 milepost 73.3, turn north on Sugarloaf Rd., go 1.5 miles to parking lot on left. GPS: 47.498036, -90.997808

Facilities: None

Size: Medium

Overnight parking: Allowed

Winter access: Unlikely

Special notes: Trailhead is adjacent to many parcels of private land.

SECTION SNAPSHOT

Trail Atlas maps: D-5, D-6

Total distance: 5.6 miles

Elevation change: A couple of smaller climbs on this section but fairly gentle overall

SHT campsites: Two

Hazards and concerns: A few short steep areas and noteworthy mud

Synopsis: Cross Sugarloaf Creek near Sugarloaf Pond, and venture along the shores of Ruffy Lake on this fairly flat section. On the north end, Dyers Creek and Two Island River are highlights.

Pro tip: Parts of this section are best enjoyed during dry periods or when the ground is frozen.

CAMPSITES

▲ **Sugarloaf Pond Campsite**
Size: Medium
Water source: Sugarloaf Pond, often stagnant and shallow and can be hard to access
Campsite has scrubby surroundings, which means a wide sky for stargazing.
3.6, 2.6 ⊕ ⊕ 3.4, 6.3

▲ **Dyers Creek Campsite**
Size: Medium
Water source: Dyers Creek or Two Island River
Campsite features a unique location between two water bodies.
6.0, 3.4 ⊕ ⊕ 2.9, 4.7

MILEAGE	Northbound	Southbound
Sugarloaf Road Trailhead	**0.0**	**5.6**
Sugarloaf Creek bridge	0.1	5.5
Sugarloaf Pond Campsite	0.9	4.7
Spur to Ruffy Lake benches	2.4	3.2
Dyers Creek bridge	4.3	1.3
Dyers Creek Campsite	4.3	1.3
Dyers Lake Road roadwalk, railroad crossing	5.1	0.5
Power line corridor	5.3	0.3
Cook County Road 1 crossing	5.4	0.2
Two Island River bridge	5.5	0.1
Cook County Road 1 Trailhead	**5.6**	**0.0**

Cook County Road 1 Trailhead to Skou Road Trailhead

Directions and GPS Waypoints: At MN-61 milepost 79.1, turn northwest on Cook Co. Rd. 1, go 3.6 miles to parking lot on right. GPS: 47.539859, -90.975425

Facilities: None

Size: Small

Overnight parking: Allowed

Winter access: No

Special notes: A short driveway leads to the lot. Please park with care so as not to block anyone else in, and use the space as efficiently as possible.

SECTION SNAPSHOT

Trail Atlas maps: D-6, D-7

Total distance: 4.9 miles (Additional 1.4-mile spur trail to Skou Road Trailhead)

Elevation change: This section fluctuates in elevation, but climbs are generally short.

SHT campsites: Five

Hazards and concerns: A few rugged climbs and unsure footing near the Cross River, an unbridged crossing at Fredenberg Creek, and steep drop-offs at overlooks

Synopsis: Climbing slowly but steadily though deciduous forest, the Superior Hiking Trail reaches Tower Overlook, descends to Fredenberg Creek and Boney's Meadow, and follows the banks of the Cross River.

Pro tip: Trail along the Cross River is surprisingly rugged, with lots of rocks and some steep areas.

- **Skou Road Trailhead.** From the main SHT, this spur trail descends 1.4 miles on a mix of hiking and ski trails. Several intersections are marked by Temperance River State Park maps. Two ski shelters are along this route.

- **Temperance River State Park Trails.** Part of this section intersects with several trails within the Temperance River State Park network. Countless loops can be created by studying a state park map. Use caution, as many winter trails are not passible when the ground is not frozen.

CAMPSITES

▲ **Fredenberg Creek Campsite**
Size: Large
Water source: Fredenberg Creek, unreliable only in extremely dry conditions
This large campsite is the best option for group use in the area.
6.3, 2.9 ⊙ ⊙ 1.8, 2.6

▲ **The Falls Campsite**
Size: Small
Water source: Cross River
Campsite is on a knob above a small waterfall. If heading south, it is not recommended to rely on space being available at this site.
4.7, 1.8 ⊙ ⊙ 0.8, 1.4

▲ **The Ledge Campsite**
Size: Small
Water source: Cross River
Campsite is, appropriately, on a skinny ledge above the river.
2.6, 0.8 ⊙ ⊙ 0.6, 0.7

▲ North Cross River Campsite

Size: Small

Water source: Cross River

Campsite is adjacent to South Cross River Campsite.

1.4; 0.6 ⊖ ⊕ 0.1, 9.0

▲ South Cross River Campsite

Size: Medium

Water source: Cross River

Campsite is next to the bridge over Cross River and North Cross River Campsite.

0.7, 0.1 ⊖ ⊕ 8.9, 11.1

MILEAGE	Northbound	Southbound
Cook County Road 1 Trailhead	**0.0**	**6.3**
Tower Overlook	1.4	4.9
Fredenberg Creek crossing	1.6	4.7
Fredenberg Creek Campsite	1.6	4.7
Boney's Meadow	2.5	3.8
Gasco Road crossing	2.6	3.7
The Falls Campsite	3.4	2.9
The Ledge Campsite	4.2	2.1
North Cross River Campsite	4.8	1.5
South Cross River Campsite	4.9	1.4
Cross River bridge	4.9	1.4
Spur to Skou Road Trailhead	4.9	1.4
Ski trail shelter	5.6	0.7
Ski trail shelter	6.0	0.3
Skou Road Trailhead	**6.3**	**0.0**

Inland to Finland

With a glance at a map of the Superior Hiking Trail, the Finland area stands out due to its wide western swing inland, far away from Lake Superior. The Trail as we know it today was not the route intended by the initial trailbuilders. Originally, the hope was to route the Superior Hiking Trail northeast from the Section 13 cliffs toward George Crosby Manitou State Park in a somewhat straight line. However, permission was not obtained from private landowners to travel along that proposed route. To avoid private lands as much as possible, the original trailbuilders created a longer but extraordinarily scenic path on the route we now enjoy. This western piece of the Superior Hiking Trail leads to two lovely lakes—it is hard to imagine the Trail without Egge and Sonju Lakes. The Section 13 Loop is a remnant of the initially-proposed route. When landowner permissions were not secured, a piece of recently-constructed Trail became a dead-end. Trailbuilders didn't want to lose the good work they'd done in the area, so they turned the dead-end into a short loop. ʌ⋀ⱴ

▊ Skou Road Trailhead to
Temperance River Wayside Trailhead

Directions and GPS Waypoints: At MN-61 milepost 78.9, turn north on Skou Rd., go 0.1 miles to parking lot on right. GPS: 47.547501, -90.895069

Facilities: None

Size: Small

Overnight parking: Allowed. Overnight parking is also allowed at nearby Temperance River Road Trailhead (At MN-61 milepost 80.2, turn north on Temperance River Rd., go 0.9 miles to parking lot on left. GPS: 47.564292, -90.88413).

Winter access: No

Special notes: Several trail intersections near the trailhead. Watch for signage to stay on the right path.

SECTION SNAPSHOT

Trail Atlas map: D-7

Total distance: 2.7 miles (Additional 1.4-mile spur trail from Skou Road, additional 0.2-mile spur trail to Temperance River Wayside Trailhead)

Elevation change: Spur trail from Skou Road Trailhead ascends steadily. On the main Superior Hiking Trail, the descent from the ridge to Temperance River Road is among the steepest on the entire Trail.

SHT campsites: None

Hazards and concerns: Steep, eroding trail near Temperance River Road.

Synopsis: A rolling, fairly easy ridgewalk with occasional glimpses of Lake Superior and Taconite Harbor descends quickly to the banks of the Temperance River, which the Trail follows into the heart of Temperance River State Park.

Pro tip: Temperance River State Park is often very busy, but the elevation change between the ridgeline and Temperance River Road keeps visitor numbers down in this area.

SPUR TRAILS

▌ **Temperance River Wayside Trailhead.** This 0.2-mile spur leads to Highway 61 and the Temperance River Wayside Trailhead.

▌ **Temperance River State Park Trails.** Part of this section intersects with several trails within the Temperance River State Park trail network. Countless loops can be created by studying a state park map. Use caution, as many winter trails are only passable when the ground is frozen.

MILEAGE	Northbound	Southbound
Skou Road Trailhead	**0.0**	**4.3**
Ski trail shelter	0.3	4.0
Ski trail shelter	0.7	3.6
Spur from Skou Road Trailhead	1.4	2.9
Vista	2.4	1.9
Temperance River Road Trailhead	3.3	1.0
Temperance River bridge	4.1	0.2
Spur to Temperance River Wayside Trailhead	4.1	0.2
Temperance River Wayside Trailhead	**4.3**	**0.0**

Temperance River Wayside Trailhead to Pincushion Mountain Trailhead

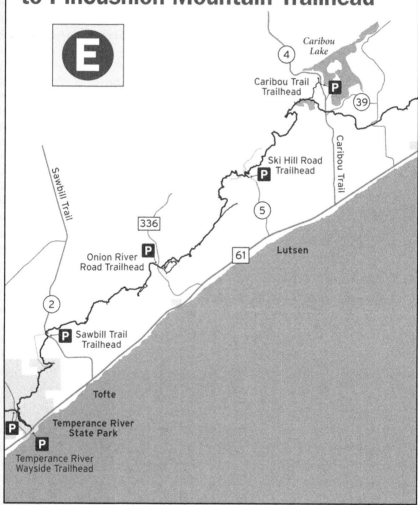

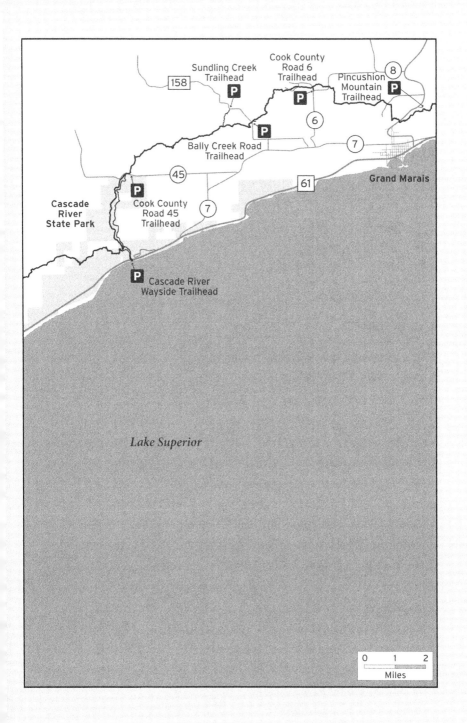

Sundling Creek Trailhead **P**

Cook County Road 6 Trailhead **P**

158

Pincushion Mountain Trailhead **P**

8

6

Bally Creek Road Trailhead

7

45

61

Grand Marais

Cascade River State Park

P Cook County Road 45 Trailhead

7

P Cascade River Wayside Trailhead

Lake Superior

0 1 2
Miles

Temperance River Wayside Trailhead to Pincushion Mountain Trailhead

█ Overview

At **Temperance River Wayside Trailhead,** a spur trail leads to the main Superior Hiking Trail, which follows Temperance River State Park trails along a stunning gorge. The Trail continues upstream along the banks of the river. A steady climb leads to perhaps the most iconic peak of the entire Superior Hiking Trail: Carlton Peak. This massive geologic formation rises dramatically above the landscape. The steep spur trail to its peak, and another to neighboring Ted Tofte Overlook, are not to be missed. The Trail descends fairly gently to Sawbill Trail.

Sawbill Trail Trailhead, also called the Britton Peak Trailhead, is part of the original section of the Superior Hiking Trail, built before the Superior Hiking Trail had been conceptualized. This section has rolling terrain with spur trails leading to overlooks. A rocky spur trail with stone steps leads to Britton Peak and affords a breathtaking view of nearby Carlton Peak. Cedar Overlook provides a view of Lake Superior. Serene Leveaux Pond sits in the shadow of Leveaux Mountain, where spur trails lead to two short loops. The Trail descends gently to Onion River toward Onion River Road.

Onion River Road Trailhead, also called Oberg Mountain Trailhead, is one of the Superior Hiking Trail's most popular trailheads. This is due to the proximity of the Oberg Mountain Loop, which features panoramic views in every direction. The Superior Hiking Trail passes the spur for the loop and continues on rolling terrain past Rollins Creek to a steep climb up the spine of Moose Mountain. The Trail here offers occasional glimpses of the surrounding landscape. A spur trail at the north end of the long ridge leads to the Lutsen Mountains ski area gondola. The Trail descends Moose Mountain and ascends Mystery Mountain. Maples thrive here, and their presence makes for a vibrant autumn experience. After descending and crossing the Poplar River on a multi-use trail, the SHT comes to two spur trails leading to Lutsen Mountains and Ski Hill Road Trailhead.

From **Ski Hill Road Trailhead,** the Superior Hiking Trail steadily ascends above the Lutsen Mountains ski area facilities to Glove Overlook before dropping into the Poplar River valley. The Trail leaves the flat stretch along the river and climbs to overlooks, including Poplar River Overlook, which highlights the oxbows of the river below. Nearby, Lake Agnes is another beautiful site with vistas like Hunters Rock. At the north end of the lake, a spur trail heads to White Sky Rock and Caribou Trail Trailhead.

The spur trail from **Caribou Trail Trailhead** leads to White Sky Rock and the junction with the main Superior Hiking Trail at Lake Agnes. Continuing around the north end of the lake, the Superior Hiking Trail crosses Caribou Trail and ascends toward Jonvick Creek. From the creek, the Trail climbs to a long ridge with only one noteworthy elevation change at the unbridged Spruce Creek. Frequent cliff edges offer inland views, followed by a descent to Indian Camp Creek. The Trail takes in Lookout Mountain's vista before dropping to the Cascade River. A spur trail leads to Cascade River Wayside Trailhead.

At **Cascade River Wayside Trailhead,** a spur trail leads to the Cascade River State Park trail network and the main Superior Hiking Trail. The Trail heads down the infamous 96 Steps wooden staircase and continues upstream along the Cascade River over many gnarled cedar roots. The Trail rises high above the river before reaching a short roadwalk on Cook County Road 45 to cross the Cascade River on a road bridge. The Cascade River Loop spur trail leads downstream on the east side of the river across from Cook County Road 45 Trailhead.

From **Cook County Road 45 Trailhead,** the Superior Hiking Trail climbs above the Cascade River once more. When it turns away from the river, the Trail passes through several open areas with multiple short ascents and descents. The SHT intersects with a spur which leads to Sundling Creek Trailhead. The Superior Hiking Trail descends to Bally Creek Road Trailhead.

Bally Creek Road Trailhead heading to Pincushion Mountain Trailhead is one of the Superior Hiking Trail's gentlest sections. After passing Bally Creek Pond, the Superior Hiking Trail arrives at Sundling Creek, where it crosses a boardwalk over a beaver dam. The forest here has an open feeling, especially when passing through the largest stand of red pines along the Trail. The pines' aroma and the needle bed are unique features of this area. Next the Superior Hiking Trail shares the North Shore State Trail for 2.5 miles where the wide path is ideal for wildlife viewing. This section of the multi-use NSST does not feature boardwalks, so conditions may be muddy. The SHT departs from the North Shore State Trail and traverses a steep hill to cross Gunflint Trail and arrive at the Pincushion Mountain Trailhead. ⋀⋀

Temperance River Wayside Trailhead to Sawbill Trail Trailhead

Directions and GPS Waypoints: At MN-61 milepost 80.3 on highway. GPS: 47.554815, -90.874025

Facilities: State park fee campsites

Size: Large

Overnight parking: No. Overnight parking is allowed within Temperance River State Park with a permit. Check in with state park staff. Overnight parking is also allowed at nearby Temperance River Road Trailhead (At MN-61 milepost 80.2, turn north on Temperance River Rd., go 0.9 miles to parking lot on left. GPS: 47.564292, -90.88413).

Winter access: Yes

Special notes: Despite its large size, this wayside may be full during peak times.

SECTION SNAPSHOT

Trail Atlas map: E-1

Total distance: 4.6 miles (Additional 0.2-mile spur trail from Temperance River Wayside Trailhead)

Elevation change: Long, fairly steady climb to Carlton Peak spur trail

SHT campsites: None

Hazards and concerns: Many rocks and roots. There is steep terrain near Carlton Peak.

Synopsis: Trail follows the scenic Temperance River, climbs Carlton Peak, and offers access to several overlooks before descending to Sawbill Trail.

Pro tip: Don't miss the often-overlooked Mediocre Overlook, or the much less mediocre Ted Tofte Overlook.

- **Mediocre Overlook.** A short 250-foot spur trail leads to an aptly-named vista. There are better places for a snack break, but this will do in a pinch.

- **Carlton Peak.** Just a short climb 0.1 miles from the main SHT is a breathtaking vista of Lake Superior and inland hills. Remnants of an old fire tower are still visible in the rock.

- **Ted Tofte Overlook.** Though not quite as high as Carlton Peak, Ted Tofte Overlook is just as gorgeous, with lake views and a good view of nearby Britton Peak. This 0.1-mile spur trail connects to a state park trail network leading to an old quarry. Use caution at intersections; the route is well-signed but can be a bit confusing.

MILEAGE	Northbound	Southbound
Temperance River Wayside Trailhead	**0.0**	**4.8**
Spur from Temperance River Wayside Trailhead	*0.2*	*4.6*
Temperance River Vista	1.4	3.4
Spur to Mediocre Overlook	*2.8*	*2.0*
Register, *spur to Carlton Peak*	3.2	1.6
Spur to Ted Tofte Overlook	*3.3*	*1.5*
Rock wall	3.4	1.4
Bench	3.8	1.0
Sawbill Trail crossing	4.6	0.2
Sawbill Trail Trailhead	**4.8**	**0.0**

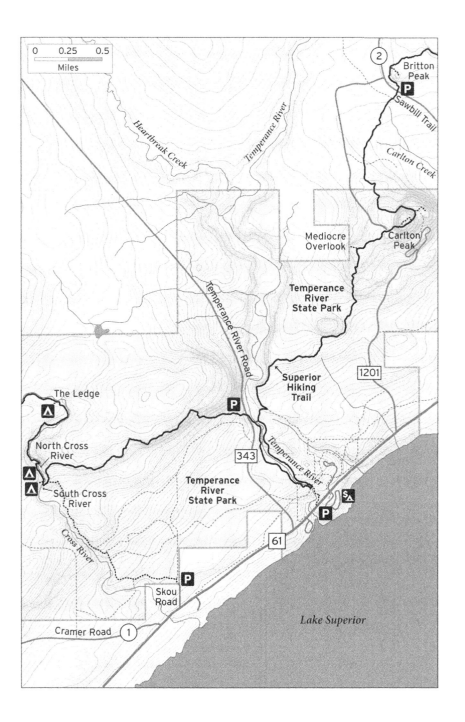

▌ Sawbill Trail Trailhead to Onion River Road Trailhead

Directions and GPS Waypoints: At MN-61 milepost 82.8, turn north on Sawbill Trail, go 2.7 miles to parking lot on right. GPS: 47.599243, -90.862695

Facilities: Toilet, kiosk

Size: Large

Overnight parking: Allowed

Winter access: Yes

Special notes: Bikers and skiers share this trailhead. Expect to encounter other users throughout much of the year, and have a backup plan to recreate elsewhere if the parking area is full.

SECTION SNAPSHOT

Trail Atlas maps: E-1, E-2

Total distance: 5.5 miles

Elevation change: Much of the elevation change on this section occurs on the several spur trails leading to vistas.

SHT campsites: Four

Hazards and concerns: There are multiple crossings of bike trails and, historically, a significant amount of mud.

Synopsis: One of the oldest sections of the Superior Hiking Trail, this section offers access to three very scenic vistas—Britton Peak, Cedar Overlook, and Leveaux Mountain—plus several streams and Leveaux Pond.

Pro tip: This is a great section to enjoy in late summer when the Trail has dried up from spring snowmelt.

SPUR TRAILS

- **Britton Peak.** Climbing for 0.1 miles up a variety of structures including many rock steps, the view from Britton Peak offers arguably the best view-to-effort ratio on the Superior Hiking Trail. The vista here showcases nearby Carlton Peak.
- **Cedar Overlook.** The view from this overlook is less impressive than its neighbors, but would be noteworthy in other sections. It's a great spot for solitude, as very few trail users take the time to explore this 450-foot spur trail.
- **Leveaux Mountain Loops.** There are two loops on Leveaux Mountain. The northern loop connects back to the main Superior Hiking Trail after 0.7 miles. The shorter, southern loop adds 0.4 miles and has wide vistas of the peaks to the southwest and views of Lake Superior. The bulk of the effort in either loop is the initial ascent up Leveaux Mountain.

CAMPSITES

▲ **Springdale Creek Campsite**
Size: Medium
Water source: Springdale Creek, unreliable in very dry conditions
Campsite is on a hill high above the creek. It is very heavily-used due to the long distance between this campsite and the Cross River campsites to the south.
9.0, 8.9 ⊕ ⊕ 2.2, 2.3

▲ **West Leveaux Pond Campsite**
Size: Medium
Water source: Leveaux Pond or Leveaux Creek (near East Leveaux Pond Campsite)
Campsite offers a good view of the nearby pond but little privacy from the Trail.
11.1, 2.2 ⊕ ⊕ 0.1, 1.3

▲ **East Leveaux Pond Campsite**

Size: Small

Water source: Leveaux Pond or nearby Leveaux Creek

Campsite has nice privacy from the Trail but limited space.

2.3, 0.1 ⊕ ⊕ 1.2, 3.2

▲ **Onion River Campsite**

Size: Large

Water source: Onion River

Though large, the campsite is frequently busy during peak times due to its proximity to a road. Campsite features a bear pole for more secure food storage.

1.3, 1.2 ⊕ ⊕ 2.0, 2.0

MILEAGE	Northbound	Southbound
Sawbill Trail Trailhead	**0.0**	**5.5**
Spur to Britton Peak	*0.0*	*5.5*
Springdale Creek bridge	1.6	3.9
Springdale Creek Campsite	1.6	3.9
Spur to Cedar Overlook	*2.9*	*2.6*
Leveaux Creek bridge	3.7	1.8
West Leveaux Campsite	3.8	1.7
East Leveaux Campsite	3.9	1.6
Spur to Leveaux Mountain Loop south junction	*4.4*	*1.1*
Spur to Leveaux Mountain Loop north junction	*4.6*	*0.9*
Onion River bridge	5.0	0.5
Onion River Campsite	5.1	0.4
Onion River Road Trailhead	**5.5**	**0.0**

Onion River Road Trailhead to Ski Hill Road Trailhead

Directions and GPS Waypoints: At MN-61 milepost 87.5, turn northwest on Onion River Rd., go 2.2 miles to parking lot on left. GPS: 47.627759, -90.783573

Facilities: Toilet, kiosk

Size: Large

Overnight parking: Allowed

Winter access: Yes

Special notes: Though large, the trailhead parking lot may be full during peak leaf peeping season.

SECTION SNAPSHOT

Trail Atlas maps: E-2, E-3

Total distance: 6.5 miles (Additional 0.2-mile spur trail to Ski Hill Road Trailhead)

Elevation change: This section has significant climbing to summit Moose and Mystery mountains alongside long and gentle stretches.

SHT campsites: Three

Hazards and concerns: Significant rocks and roots. Steep climbs often have uneven footing.

Synopsis: This section offers access to the scenic Oberg Mountain Loop, climbs Moose Mountain, descends into the headwaters of Rollins Creek, and climbs Mystery Mountain.

CAMPSITES

▲ **West Rollins Creek Campsite**

Size: Medium

Water source: Rollins Creek

Campsite, slightly larger than its neighbor, is in a pleasant wooded area not far from the creek.

3.2, 2.0 ⊕ ➔ 0.0, 4.4

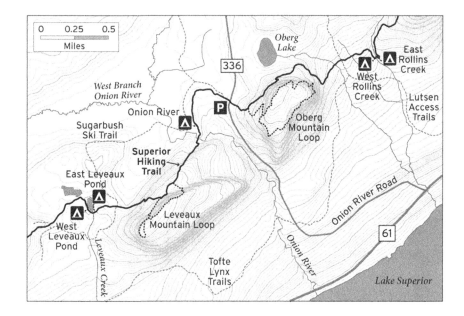

CAMPSITES, continued

▲ **East Rollins Creek Campsite**
Size: Small
Water source: Rollins Creek
Campsite is situated along the banks of Rollins Creek.
2.0, 0.0 ⊖ ⊕ 4.4, 6.5

▲ **Mystery Mountain Campsite**
Size: Large
No water source. Nearest source is 0.5 miles north at the Poplar River. Please use extreme caution if you choose to have a fire; carry enough water to thoroughly douse any embers.
Campsite is located in a maple forest with spectacular fall colors.
4.4, 4.4 ⊖ ⊕ 2.1, 2.5

MILEAGE	Northbound	Southbound
Onion River Road Trailhead	**0.0**	**6.7**
Spur to Oberg Mountain Loop	0.2	6.5
West Rollins Creek Campsite	1.6	5.1
Rollins Creek bridge	1.6	5.1
East Rollins Creek Campsite	1.6	5.1
Ridgetop Vista	2.3	4.4
Spur to Lutsen gondola	3.4	3.3
Vista	5.1	1.6
Mystery Mountain Campsite	6.0	0.7
Poplar River bridge	6.5	0.2
Two spurs to Ski Hill Road Trailhead	6.5	0.2
Ski Hill Road Trailhead	**6.7**	**0.0**

The Superior Trail Races

Since 1991, the Superior Hiking Trail has hosted the annual Superior 100 Mile Trail Race, a unique endurance event that pushes participants to traverse some of the finest sections of the Trail. The race is organized by Rocksteady Running, a private racing company that coordinates with the Association and land management agencies to permit the event. It has grown to include races of shorter distances as well as a spring race event. Over the years, these races have attracted thousands of participants from all over the country to experience the joys and challenges of the Trail.

While there are several events that take place on the Superior Hiking Trail each year, the Superior Trail Races stand out for their dedication to giving back to the Trail. Donations and memberships from race organizers and participants have totalled in the tens of thousands of dollars, and many have volunteered with the Association to help with maintenance and trail improvement projects—a few have even joined the Association's Board of Directors. ⚲⚲

Ski Hill Road Trailhead to Caribou Trail Trailhead

BEGINNING TRAILHEAD

Directions and GPS Waypoints: At MN-61 milepost 90.1, turn north on Ski Hill Rd., go 3.2 miles to parking lot on left. GPS: 47.666161, -90.719028

Facilities: None

Size: Small

Overnight parking: Allowed

Winter access: Yes

Special notes: There are two parking options in this area. The preferred option is an extremely small trailhead located at the start of the spur trail to the main Superior Hiking Trail. If this parking area is full, additional parking can be found in a nearby lot closer to the core of the Lutsen Mountains ski area complex. Please abide by any posted signs regarding parking.

SECTION SNAPSHOT

Trail Atlas map: E-3

Total distance: 5.5 miles (Additional 0.2-mile spur trail from Ski Hill Road Trailhead, 0.9-mile spur trail to Caribou Trail Trailhead)

Elevation change: This section has several noteworthy climbs mixed with low-lying flat areas.

SHT campsites: Four

Hazards and concerns: Several steep, uneven staircases. Use caution when crossing Caribou Trail.

Synopsis: This section explores the beauty surrounding Lutsen, from great inland overlooks to time along the Poplar River and Lake Agnes.

Pro tip: This section is bookended by two overlooks—Glove Overlook in the south and White Sky Rock in the north. Either one makes a fabulous, quick trip for exceptional views.

▮ **Caribou Trail Trailhead.** A spur trail leads 0.8 miles to another short spur trail to White Sky Rock and an additional 0.1 miles to the Caribou Trail Trailhead.

CAMPSITES

▲ **West Poplar River Campsite**
Size: Medium
Water source: Poplar River
Sitting on a hill above the river, this campsite is better suited for hammocks than tents due to its slope.
6.5, 2.1 ⊛ ⊛ 0.4, 3.3

▲ **East Poplar River Campsite**
Size: Small
Water source: Poplar River
Campsite is smaller but flatter than its neighbor.
2.5, 0.4 ⊛ ⊛ 2.9, 3.3

▲ **West Lake Agnes Campsite**
Size: Medium
Water source: Lake Agnes
Sitting high on a hill above Lake Agnes, this campsite is the best option for groups in this area. Campsite features a bear pole for more secure food storage.
3.3, 2.9 ⊛ ⊛ 0.4, 2.7

▲ **East Lake Agnes Campsite**
Size: Medium
Water source: Lake Agnes
Overused campsite is in high demand due to its proximity to Lake Agnes. Be prepared to share the campsite with fellow campers; it is among the most used campsites on the Trail. During peak times, consider camping elsewhere to avoid overuse of the site. Campsite features a bear pole for more secure food storage.
3.3, 0.4 ⊛ ⊛ 2.3, 4.5

MILEAGE	Northbound	Southbound
Ski Hill Road Trailhead	**0.0**	**6.6**
Two spurs from Ski Hill Road Trailhead	*0.2*	*6.4*
Lutsen Overlook	0.4	6.2
Lutsen trail crossing	1.3	5.3
Glove Overlook	1.5	5.1
West Poplar River Campsite	1.8	4.8
Snowmobile trail crossing	2.1	4.5
East Poplar River Campsite	2.2	4.4
Poplar River vista	4.5	2.1
Agnes Creek bridge	5.1	1.5
West Lake Agnes Campsite	5.1	1.5
Hunters Rock, register	5.4	1.2
East Lake Agnes Campsite	5.5	1.1
Spur to Caribou Trail Trailhead and White Sky Rock	*5.7*	*0.9*
Spur to White Sky Rock	*6.5*	*0.1*
Caribou Trail Trailhead	**6.6**	**0.0**

▌ Caribou Trail Trailhead to Cascade River Wayside Trailhead

Directions and GPS Waypoints: At MN-61 milepost 92.0, turn north on Caribou Trail, go 4.1 miles to Co. Rd. 94. Turn east, take immediate left to parking lot. GPS: 47.707174, -90.667417

Facilities: None

Size: Small

Overnight Parking: Allowed

Winter access: Yes

Special notes: This small trailhead may be full during peak times.

SECTION SNAPSHOT

Trail Atlas maps: E-3, E-4, E-5

Total distance: 9.5 miles (Additional 0.9-mile spur trail from Caribou Trail Trailhead, 0.4-mile spur trail to Cascade River Wayside Trailhead)

Elevation change: This section has several significant climbs, most notably to reach the Spruce Creek ridgeline and in the vicinity of Lookout Mountain.

SHT campsites: Three

Hazards and concerns: Use caution when crossing Caribou Trail. Be careful on several steep, uneven staircases and slopes. Spruce Creek is unbridged but can generally be crossed except under extremely wet conditions.

Synopsis: A long, scenic section follows the northern shoreline of Lake Agnes, crosses Jonvick Creek and then ascends to a long ridge with several views. Spruce Creek and Indian Camp Creek are highlights of this section, as is Lookout Mountain with its dramatic vista. The Trail descends ruggedly to the Cascade River.

Pro tip: Few sections are as colorful as this one in autumn.

- **Caribou Trail Trailhead.** A spur trail leads 0.1 miles to another spur trail to White Sky Rock and an additional 0.8 miles to the main Superior Hiking Trail.
- **Jerry Evjen's Overlook.** Vista is worth the 60-foot detour.
- **Cascade River State Park Trails.** Part of this section intersects with several trails within the extensive Cascade River State Park network. Countless loops can be created by studying a state park map.
- **Cascade River Wayside Trailhead.** A spur trail follows state park trails 0.4 miles to a state park bridge over the Cascade River and an additional 0.2 miles to the Cascade River Wayside Trailhead.

CAMPSITES

▲ **Jonvick Creek Campsite**
Size: Small
Water source: Beaver pond
Small campsite offers access to wildlife viewing at the small beaver pond.
2.7, 2.3 ⊛ ⊛ 2.2, 5.4

▲ **Spruce Creek Campsite**
Size: Large
Water source: Spruce Creek
Set among cedars and along the banks of Spruce Creek, campsite is lovely but involves a very steep climb to the latrine.
4.5, 2.2 ⊛ ⊛ 3.2, 6.2

▲ **Camp Creek Campsite**
Size: Large
Water source: Indian Camp Creek
Airy campsite mysteriously has two latrines.
5.4, 3.2 ⊛ ⊛ 3.0, 3.5

MILEAGE	Northbound	Southbound
Caribou Trail Trailhead	**0.0**	**11.0**
Spur to White Sky Rock	*0.1*	*10.9*
Spur from Caribou Trail Trailhead and White Sky Rock	*0.9*	*10.1*
Caribou Trail crossing	1.7	9.3
Cook County Road 39 crossing	1.8	9.2
Private benches	2.1	8.9
Jonvick Creek Campsite	3.0	8.0
Boardwalk over beaver dam	3.0	8.0
Hall Road crossing	3.7	7.3
Spruce Creek crossing	5.2	5.8
Spruce Creek Campsite	5.2	5.8
Lutsen Trail east end	6.7	4.3
Spur to Jerry Evjen's Overlook	*7.1*	*3.9*
Lutsen (snowmobile) Trail east end	7.2	3.8
Indian Camp Creek bridge	8.4	2.6
Camp Creek Campsite	8.4	2.6
Lookout Mountain, state park campsite 5, fee and reservation required	9.5	1.5
Cascade Creek bridge	10.1	0.9
Spur to Cascade River bridge, Cascade River Loop spur south junction, and Cascade River Wayside Trailhead	*10.4*	*0.6*
Bridge over Cascade River, Cascade River Loop spur south junction	*10.8*	*0.2*
Cascade River Wayside Trailhead	**11.0**	**0.0**

Cascade River Wayside Trailhead to Cook County Road 45 Trailhead

BEGINNING TRAILHEAD

Directions and GPS Waypoints: At MN-61 milepost 99.9 on north side of highway. GPS: 47.706943, -90.524638

Facilities: State park fee campsites nearby

Size: Medium

Overnight parking: No. Overnight parking is allowed within Cascade River State Park with a permit. Check in with state park staff.

Winter access: Yes

Special notes: Easier access to the main Superior Hiking Trail is available from the parking lot within Cascade River State Park. Permit required for day and overnight parking inside the park.

SECTION SNAPSHOT

Trail Atlas map: E-5

Total distance: 3.0 miles (Additional 0.6-mile spur trail from Cascade River Wayside Trailhead)

Elevation change: This section is surprisingly rugged as it ascends and descends, often steeply, along many drainages around the Cascade River.

SHT campsites: Three

Hazards and concerns: Be careful on several steep, uneven staircases and slopes, and mindful of a few aging trail structures. Pay attention to your surroundings on the Cook County Road 45 roadwalk.

Synopsis: Trail features many viewpoints of scenic waterfalls along the spur to the Cascade River Wayside Trailhead. The main SHT descends the infamous 96 Steps wooden staircase and follows the river closely before climbing from the bottom of the river valley through a stand of maple trees. A short roadwalk along Cook County Road 45 crosses the Cascade River on the way to the trailhead.

Pro tip: Combined with the Cascade River Loop Spur, this section is part of the Cascade River Loop.

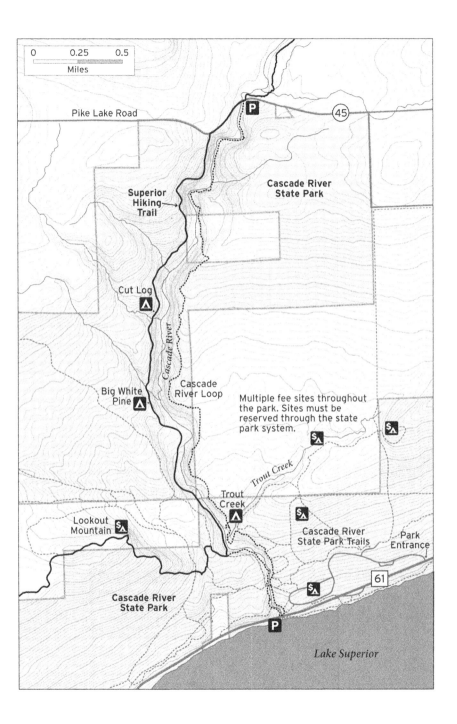

- **Cascade River Wayside Trailhead.** Spur trail follows state park trails 0.2 miles to a state park bridge over the Cascade River and an additional 0.4 miles to the main SHT.
- **Cascade River State Park Trails.** Part of this section intersects with several trails within the extensive Cascade River State Park network. Countless loops can be created by studying a state park map.
- **Cascade River Loop Spur.** A 3.5-mile spur trail makes up the eastern half of the Cascade River Loop. The crossing of Trout Creek is unbridged, but generally easy to cross except after a large rain event or during snowmelt.

CAMPSITES

▲ **Big White Pine Campsite**
Size: Small
Water source: Cascade River tributary
Campsite sits among many large pines and is busy during peak times.
6.2, 3.0 ⊕ ⊕ 0.5, 2.9

▲ **Cut Log Campsite**
Size: Small
Water source: Small creek
Campsite is named for the remnants of long-ago logging.
3.5, 0.5 ⊕ ⊕ 2.4, 6.4

▲ **Trout Creek Campsite**
Size: Large
Water source: Trout Creek or Cascade River
Campsite is located on the Cascade River Loop Spur Trail and is not easily accessible to those traversing the main Superior Hiking Trail.

MILEAGE	Northbound	Southbound
Cascade River Wayside Trailhead	**0.0**	**3.6**
Bridge over Cascade River, Cascade River Loop spur south junction	*0.2*	*3.4*
Spur trail from Cascade River Wayside Trailhead	*0.6*	*3.0*
96 Steps	0.6	3.0
Big White Pine Campsite	1.6	2.0
Cut Log Campsite	2.1	1.5
Waterfall vista	3.2	0.4
Cook County Road 45 roadwalk west end	3.3	0.3
Cook County Road 45 roadwalk east end	3.6	0.0
Cook County Road 45 Trailhead	**3.6**	**0.0**

▌Cook County Road 45 Trailhead to Bally Creek Road Trailhead

Directions and GPS Waypoints: At MN-61 milepost 101.7, turn north on Co. Rd. 7, go 2.0 miles to junction with Cook Co. Rd. 44. Continue on Co. Rd. 44 for 0.5 miles. Turn west on Co. Rd. 45, go 2.6 miles to parking lot on right. GPS: 47.746362, -90.523629

Facilities: None

Size: Medium

Overnight parking: Allowed

Winter access: No. Nearby winter access is available at the multi-use Sundling Creek Trailhead.

Special notes: The Superior Hiking Trail leading south from Cook County Road 45 Trailhead requires a short roadwalk west across the county road bridge. Overnight parking is also available at the Sundling Creek Trailhead (At MN-61 milepost 101.7, turn north on Co. Rd. 7, go 4.3 miles. Turn north on Co. Rd. 48, go 0.3 miles. Turn left on Bally Creek Rd., go 1.9 miles to grassy parking lot on left. GPS: 47.773982, -90.451240)

SECTION SNAPSHOT

Trail Atlas maps: E-5, E-6

Total distance: 5.5 miles

Elevation change: There are multiple climbs and descents on this section.

SHT campsites: Two

Hazards and concerns: Due to the forest type and various logging efforts over the years, this section is brushier than surrounding sections.

Synopsis: Trail climbs high above the Cascade River before heading away from it over a series of hills.

Pro tip: This section typically offers more solitude than the popular Cascade River area to the south.

■ **Sundling Creek.** A spur trail leads off the ridge from the main Superior Hiking Trail. In 0.5 miles it comes to Sundling Creek Campsite. After 0.7 miles it arrives at Sundling Creek Trailhead.

CAMPSITES

▲ **North Cascade River Campsite**
Size: Large
Water source: Cascade River
Campsite sits high above the river and has a trail register.
2.9, 2.4 ⊖ ⊕ 4.0, 4.7

▲ **Sundling Creek Campsite**
Size: Medium
Water source: Sundling Creek
Grassy campsite on a long spur trail 0.5 miles from the main SHT.
6.4, 4.0 ⊖ ⊕ 1.7, 1.9

MILEAGE	Northbound	Southbound
Cook County Road 45 Trailhead	**0.0**	**5.5**
Minnow Trap Creek bridge	0.1	5.4
North Cascade River Campsite, register	0.9	4.6
Spur to Sundling Creek Campsite and Sundling Creek Trailhead	*4.4*	*1.1*
Bally Creek Road Trailhead	**5.5**	**0.0**

▋ Bally Creek Road Trailhead to Pincushion Mountain Trailhead

Directions and GPS Waypoints: At MN-61 milepost 101.7, turn north on Cook Co. Rd. 7 and go 4.3 miles. Turn north on Cook Co. Rd. 48, go 0.3 miles. Turn left on Bally Creek Rd, go 1.0 mile to parking lot on left. GPS: 47.767554, -90.436305

Facilities: None

Size: Small

Overnight parking: Allowed

Winter access: No. Nearby winter access is available at the multi-use Sundling Creek Trailhead.

Special notes: The parking lot is extremely small and located on a road frequented by logging trucks. Please do not park outside the trailhead. Overnight parking is also available at the Cook County Road 6 Trailhead (At MN-61 milepost 101.7, turn north on Cook Co. Rd. 7, go 6.0 miles. Turn north on Cook Co. Rd. 6, go 1.5 miles to pull-through parking lot at intersection with 115F. GPS: 47.781019, -90.392682)

SECTION SNAPSHOT

Trail Atlas maps: E-6, E-7

Total distance: 8.2 miles

Elevation change: The section is predominantly flat, other than an extremely steep section between a ridge and Pincushion Mountain Trailhead.

SHT campsites: Two

Hazards and concerns: There is aging boardwalk infrastructure on this section, along with frequent logging activity, a multi-use trail corridor, and steep elevation change south of Pincushion Mountain Trailhead.

Synopsis: This fairly flat section features beaver ponds, boardwalks, and red pines.

Pro tip: A long wet area along the shared route on the North Shore State Trail is most enjoyable when the ground is frozen.

■ **Cook County Road 6 Trailhead.** At the northernmost U.S. Forest Service Road 115F crossing, follow the narrow forest road 0.1 miles south to reach the Cook County Road 6 Trailhead.

CAMPSITES

▲ **South Bally Creek Pond Campsite**
Size: Medium
Water source: Beaver pond, often stagnant in late summer
Campsite receives heavy use, particularly during peak times, due to its proximity to a road.
4.7, 1.7 ⊕ ⊛ 0.2, 10.8

▲ **North Bally Creek Pond Campsite**
Size: Small
Water source: Beaver pond, often stagnant in late summer
Campsite, more sloped than its neighbor, is a bit farther from the road and receives slightly less traffic.
1.9, 0.2 ⊕ ⊛ 10.6, 10.7

MILEAGE	Northbound	Southbound
Bally Creek Road Trailhead	**0.0**	**8.2**
South Bally Creek Pond Campsite	0.1	8.1
North Bally Creek Pond Campsite	0.3	7.9
Sundling Creek boardwalk	0.9	7.3
Southernmost USFS 115F crossing	2.1	6.1
Northernmost USFS 115F crossing, *spur to Cook County Road 6 Trailhead*	*3.1*	*5.1*
Cook County Road 6 crossing	3.6	4.6
North Shore State Trail west end	3.8	4.4
Old Ski Hill Road crossing	6.2	2.0
North Shore State Trail east end	6.3	1.9
Gunflint Trail crossing	7.2	1.0
Pincushion Mountain Trailhead	**8.2**	**0.0**

Pincushion Mountain Trailhead to Northern Terminus

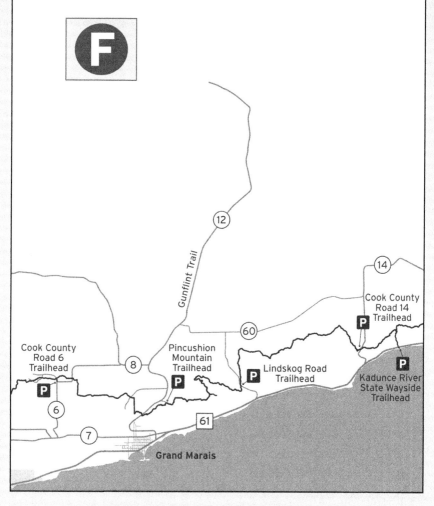

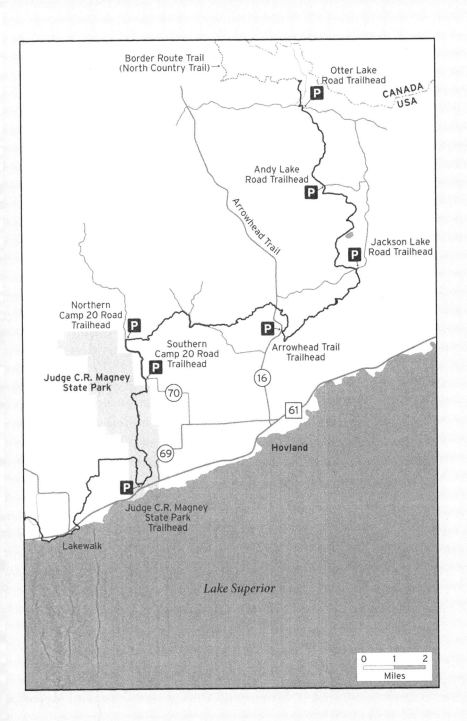

Pincushion Mountain Trailhead to Northern Terminus

█ Overview

Pincushion Mountain Trailhead showcases a sustainable footpath to Pincushion Mountain, one of the most beloved peaks of the North Shore. The Superior Hiking Trail descends steeply to the banks of the Devil Track River and to a remarkable bridge over its rushing waters. The Trail climbs above the Devil Track River gorge to a view of Devil Track Falls far below before descending through a pine forest.

At **Lindskog Road Trailhead,** the Superior Hiking Trail climbs along Woods Creek into a maple forest punctuated by rare meadows where wildflowers and vistas abound. The Trail navigates many small drainages, giving this section a roller-coaster feel. This section has rhyolite rock shards making up parts of the tread. Descending toward Kimball Creek, the Trail follows the shoulder of its ridge before crossing two of its branches. An extremely steep but quick ascent brings the Trail away from the creek.

From **Cook County Road 14 Trailhead,** the Trail's rocky tread passes through deep forests with occasional glimpses of Lake Superior before arriving at Stone Creek. This creek, known for many years as Crow Creek, features a sturdy bridge. A twin bridge is located nearby, crossing the West Fork of the Kadunce River over a narrow, deeply-incised gorge. The gentle path leads to the Kadunce River and a spur trail downhill to Highway 61.

At the **Kadunce River State Wayside Trailhead,** a spur trail leads uphill along the Kadunce River and its gorge. The Superior Hiking Trail continues to follow the river upstream before climbing to a forested knob. Descending, the Trail arrives at the lowest point along the Superior Hiking Trail at the Lakewalk. The route along Lake Superior's shore is flat but very challenging: the small rocks slide around and water levels may necessitate retreating into the nearby scrubby forest. Even so, this intimate lake experience is worth the effort. After leaving the Lakewalk, the Trail crosses Hane Creek and makes a slow ascent into the Little Brule River valley, then follows property lines straight into Judge C.R. Magney State Park.

After departing the **Judge C.R. Magney State Park Trailhead,** the Superior Hiking Trail passes one of the wonders of the North Shore: Devil's Kettle. This famous waterfall on the Brule River can be viewed from several spots. Few state park visitors venture past Devil's Kettle where the SHT continues along the Brule River before climbing away from the river to Bald Hill Vista. A bridge across the Flute Reed River brings the Trail to Southern Camp 20 Trailhead where the longest roadwalk of the Superior Hiking Trail begins, extending 1.7 miles.

From **Northern Camp 20 Road Trailhead,** the Superior Hiking Trail enters a long stretch of low-lying terrain where private lands are dotted with logging activity and replanted areas. This is prime moose habitat. The Trail crosses small tributaries of the Flute Reed River and arrives at rustic Tom Lake Road (a wide trail), which it follows for over a mile. Where a pond has flooded the road, an optional, extremely rugged route bypasses the wet area. The Trail climbs steeply away from Tom Lake Road, past South Carlson Pond, and through a low, brushy area before crossing Arrowhead Trail. The SHT skirts North Carlson Pond and arrives at a spur trail and bridge which lead to Arrowhead Trail Trailhead.

A short spur trail from **Arrowhead Trail Trailhead** descends to a bridge over Carlson Creek to the junction with the main Superior Hiking Trail. The Trail ascends dramatically to a long ridgeline with many views. The ridge breaks near a pond, then resumes before arriving at another large beaver pond. A steep climb brings the Trail to Hellacious Overlook, a long vista of Lake Superior, Isle Royale, and Farquhar Peak. Heading into a low area before a final climb, the Trail finally descends to Jackson Lake Road.

Jackson Lake Road Trailhead is northeast of where the Superior Hiking Trail crosses the road. The Trail gently ascends, reaching a long puncheon (a simple boardwalk) through a cedar swamp, one of the longest structures on the entire Trail. A glacial erratic and Jackson Creek are highlights of this remote area. The Trail ascends to a series of rock outcroppings and arrives at Rosebush Ridge, the highest point on the Superior Hiking Trail at 1,829 feet. While there is no view from this wooded location, a narrow vista with a bench is just a mile north. From there the Trail descends to Andy Lake Road.

Andy Lake Road Trailhead begins one of the flattest sections of the Superior Hiking Trail. Open meadows from past and present logging mean an ever-evolving forest and great potential to spot wildlife. As the Trail nears its final trailhead, it shares logging roads.

Otter Lake Road Trailhead is the northernmost trailhead for the Superior Hiking Trail and was, for many years, the northern terminus. A much more noteworthy northern terminus is now a mile beyond Otter Lake Road; it is accessible through an out-and-back excursion, much like the Trail's southern terminus. After following Otter Lake Road across the Swamp River, the Superior Hiking Trail shares the Border Route Trail for a climb to 270 Degree Overlook. Here the panorama includes the wilderness of Canada to the north. The Pigeon River, marking the border between Minnesota and Ontario, Canada is mostly hidden by trees, but can be heard if it's not too windy. To the south, the Swamp River curves and distant ridges rise above the flatlands. ⋀⋀

Pincushion Mountain Trailhead to Lindskog Road Trailhead

Directions and GPS Waypoints: At MN-61 milepost 110.0, turn north on Gunflint Trail, go 2.0 miles. Turn southeast on Pincushion Drive, go 0.25 miles to parking lot. GPS: 47.771035, -90.317319

Facilities: Toilet, kiosk

Size: Large

Overnight parking: Allowed

Winter access: Yes

Special notes: Multiple trail networks leave from this trailhead. Stay off groomed ski trails in the winter.

SECTION SNAPSHOT

Trail Atlas maps: F-1, F-2

Total distance: 4.8 miles

Elevation change: Trail is fairly gentle between Pincushion Mountain Trailhead and the spur trail to the summit. North of the spur trail there is significant elevation change down to Devil Track River and up again to the Lindskog Road Trailhead.

SHT campsites: Two

Hazards and concerns: Rocky spur trail to Pincushion Mountain Overlook, steep terrain and cliff edges

Synopsis: The first miles from Pincushion Mountain Trailhead showcase some of the most sustainably-built Superior Hiking Trail. A spur trail leads to the awe-inspiring Pincushion Mountain Overlook. The Trail follows and crosses the Devil Track River, then climbs to several views into the Devil Track gorge.

Pro tip: Don't underestimate the difficulty of the northern half of this section—it's much harder than the southern half!

SPUR TRAIL

- **Pincushion Mountain Overlook.** A 0.25-mile spur trail leads up and over a rock face to amazing views of Lake Superior, Grand Marais, the Sawtooth Mountains, and Wildflower Hill.

CAMPSITES

▲ **West Devil Track River Campsite**
Size: Large
Water source: Devil Track River
Campsite is located next to the A-frame bridge over the river. This large site is the best option for group use in this section.
10.8, 10.6 ⊖ ⊕ 0.1, 2.6

▲ **East Devil Track River Campsite**
Size: Small
Water source: Devil Track River
Small campsite sits on a narrow ledge above the river.
10.7, 0.1 ⊖ ⊕ 2.5, 4.9

MILEAGE	Northbound	Southbound
Pincushion Mountain Trailhead	**0.0**	**4.8**
Spur to Pincushion Mountain Overlook	*1.8*	*3.0*
Ski trail crossing	2.3	2.5
Bench at top of hill	2.4	2.4
West Devil Track Campsite	2.7	2.1
Register, Devil Track River bridge	2.7	2.1
East Devil Track Campsite	2.8	2.0
Spruce Knob	2.9	1.9
Devil Track Falls vista, bench	4.0	0.8
Devil Track Creek bridge	4.5	0.3
Lindskog Road Trailhead	**4.8**	**0.0**

Lindskog Road Trailhead to Cook County Road 14 Trailhead

Directions and GPS Waypoints: At MN-61 milepost 113.8, turn north, go 0.8 miles to parking lot on left. GPS: 47.778040, -90.265563

Facilities: None

Size: Medium

Overnight parking: Allowed

Winter access: No

Special notes: Expect to encounter other users throughout much of the year, and have a backup plan to recreate elsewhere if the parking lot is full. More space can be found at Pincushion Mountain Trailhead.

SECTION SNAPSHOT

Trail Atlas maps: F-2, F-3

Total distance: 6.6 miles

Elevation change: Dramatic climbs on both ends of this section, plus passing through many drainages, give a feeling of constantly changing elevation.

SHT campsites: Four

Hazards and concerns: In winter, the route across Wildflower Hill is not clear due to lack of trees to sign. The Trail is steep and eroding near Kimball Creek.

Synopsis: This diverse section highlights several scenic creeks and views from Wildflower Hill.

Pro tip: The many campsites on this section are a great place to take a break from the climbing and descending.

▲ **Woods Creek Campsite**

Size: Medium

Water source: Woods Creek

Campsite is frequently busy during peak times due to its proximity to a road.

2.6, 2.5 ⊕ ⊕ 2.4, 3.5

▲ **Durfee Creek Campsite**

Size: Large

Water source: Durfee Creek, located north of the campsite down a significant hill. Southbound trail users should fill up with water before climbing the hill to the campsite.

Campsite sits high above Durfee Creek with a wide range of tent pads to choose from.

4.9, 2.4 ⊕ ⊕ 1.1, 3.6

▲ **Cliff Creek Campsite**

Size: Large

Water source: Cliff Creek

Campsite is along the banks of the small but scenic creek.

3.5, 1.1 ⊕ ⊕ 2.5, 3.7

▲ **Kimball Creek Campsite**

Size: Small

Water source: Kimball Creek

Campsite is located near bridges over branches of Kimball Creek. Campsite is frequently busy during peak times due to its proximity to a road.

3.6, 2.5 ⊕ ⊕ 1.2, 1.5

MILEAGE	Northbound	Southbound
Lindskog Road Trailhead	**0.0**	**6.6**
Lindskog Road crossing	0.0	6.6
Woods Creek Campsite	0.5	6.1
Wildflower Hill	2.4	4.2
Durfee Creek Campsite	2.9	3.7
Durfee Creek bridge	3.0	3.6
Cliff Creek Campsite	4.0	2.6
Scrub Oak Vista	5.0	1.6
Kimball Creek bridge	6.5	0.1
Kimball Creek Campsite	6.5	0.1
Kimball Creek Trail intersection	6.5	0.1
Cook County Road 14 Trailhead	**6.6**	**0.0**

Cook County Road 14 Trailhead to Kadunce River State Wayside Trailhead

Directions and GPS Waypoints: At MN-61 milepost 117.6, turn north, go 0.7 miles to pull-through parking lot on left. GPS: 47.793328, -90.182649

Facilities: None

Size: Medium

Overnight parking: Allowed

Winter access: No

Special notes: Unique drive-through trailhead requires thoughtful parking. Do not block the road in or out.

SECTION SNAPSHOT

Trail Atlas map: F-3

Total distance: 1.7 miles (Additional 0.7-mile spur trail to Kadunce River State Wayside Trailhead)

Elevation change: A very gentle section; the spur trail to Kadunce River State Wayside is a prolonged elevation change.

SHT campsites: Two

Hazards and concerns: Steep gorge near both branches of the Kadunce River

Synopsis: A short section features three impressive bridges, including one over the deep, narrow West Fork of the Kadunce River gorge.

Pro tip: Several private trails connect to the Superior Hiking Trail in this section. Please pay attention and follow signage to remain on the SHT to avoid trespassing on private property.

SPUR TRAIL

■ **Kadunce River State Wayside Trailhead.** A 0.7-mile spur trail connects the Superior Hiking Trail with the Kadunce River State Wayside Trailhead, a parking lot located on the shore of Lake Superior. The spur trail follows spectacular views of this wild North Shore river. Note that on certain maps, this parking area is referred to as the

Kodunce River State Wayside. Local signage favors the Kadunce spelling.

CAMPSITES

▲ **Crow Creek Campsite**
Size: Medium
Water source: Stone Creek, most accessible near the bridge site downstream
Campsite sits along the banks of Stone Creek. This creek was called Crow Creek by the SHTA for years, but recent updates to map data have confirmed that the name of the creek is actually Stone Creek.
3.7, 1.2 ⊖ ⊕ 0.3, 0.8

▲ **West Fork Kadunce Campsite**
Size: Medium
Water source: Nearby, but not at site. Campsite is located above a gorge, so water is audible but not accessible. Plan to get water at Stone Creek to the south or from the Kadunce River to the north. This campsite features less privacy than most campsites.
1.5, 0.3 ⊖ ⊕ 0.5, 5.7

MILEAGE	Northbound	Southbound
Cook County Road 14 Trailhead	**0.0**	**2.4**
Cook County Road 14 crossing	0.0	2.4
Power line corridor	0.2	2.2
Stone Creek bridge	1.1	1.3
Crow Creek Campsite	1.1	1.3
West Fork Kadunce bridge	1.4	1.0
West Fork Kadunce Campsite	1.4	1.0
Kadunce River bridge	1.7	0.7
Spur to Kadunce River Wayside Trailhead	*1.7*	*0.7*
Kadunce River Wayside Trailhead	**2.4**	**0.0**

▌ Kadunce River State Wayside Trailhead to Judge C.R. Magney State Park Trailhead

BEGINNING TRAILHEAD

Directions and GPS Waypoints: At MN-61 milepost 119 on south side of highway. GPS: 47.794024, -90.154132

Facilities: None

Size: Medium

Overnight parking: No

Winter access: Yes

Special notes: This trailhead is popular for trail access and Lake Superior access.

SECTION SNAPSHOT

Trail Atlas map: F-4

Total distance: 9.1 miles (Additional 0.7-mile spur trail from Kadunce River State Wayside Trailhead)

Elevation change: While there are some gentle portions of this section, long stretches involve changing elevation.

SHT campsites: Four

Hazards and concerns: Use caution at three crossings of Highway 61. The route along Lake Superior may be wet or dangerous in inclement weather.

Synopsis: Trail follows the Kadunce River upstream, then ascends to a ridge before dropping down to the Lakewalk along Lake Superior. The Trail ascends to the Little Brule River before crossing into Judge C.R. Magney State Park.

Pro tip: The Lakewalk is flat but extremely challenging to walk on, given the millions of tiny rocks that make up the shoreline. The Trail turns north away from the lake just past a small island.

▪ **Kadunce River State Wayside.** A 0.7-mile spur trail connects the main Superior Hiking Trail with the Kadunce River State Wayside, a parking lot located on the shore of Lake Superior. The spur trail follows spectacular views of this wild North Shore river. Note that on certain maps, this parking area is referred to as the Kodunce River State Wayside. Local signage favors the Kadunce spelling.

CAMPSITES

▲ **Kadunce River Campsite**
Size: Small
Water source: Kadunce River
Campsite is nestled in the woods above the Kadunce River.
0.8, 0.5 ⊕ ⊕ 5.2, 5.6

▲ **South Little Brule River Campsite**
Size: Small
Water source: Little Brule River, unreliable during dry conditions
Campsite is the first that northbound trail users encounter.
5.7, 5.2 ⊕ ⊕ 0.4, 0.4

▲ **North Little Brule River Campsite**
Size: Medium
Water source: Little Brule River, unreliable during dry conditions
Campsite is on the bank of a scenic stream.
5.6, 0.4 ⊕ ⊕ 0.0, 11.7

▲ **Northwest Little Brule River Campsite**
Size: Small
Water source: Little Brule River, unreliable during dry conditions
Campsite is the first that southbound hikers encounter after a long stretch without campsites.
0.4, 0.0 ⊕ ⊕ 11.7, 14.5

MILEAGE	Northbound	Southbound
Kadunce River Wayside Trailhead	**0.0**	**9.8**
Spur from Kadunce River Wayside Trailhead, register	*0.7*	*9.1*
Kadunce River Campsite	0.9	8.9
Timber Wolf Creek	2.3	7.5
Kelley's Hill Road crossing	2.6	7.2
Lakewalk west end	3.2	6.6
Lakewalk east end	4.6	5.2
Hane Creek bridge	4.9	4.9
South Little Brule River Campsite	6.1	3.7
North Little Brule River Campsite	6.5	3.3
Northwest Little Brule River Campsite	6.5	3.3
Gauthier Road crossing (private road)	7.0	2.8
Judge C.R. Magney State Park Trailhead	**9.8**	**0.0**

Judge C.R. Magney State Park Trailhead to Northern Camp 20 Road Trailhead

BEGINNING TRAILHEAD

Directions and GPS Waypoints: At MN-61 milepost 123.8, turn north into state park, continue on park road to parking lot. GPS: 47.819763, -90.053463

Facilities: Toilet, running water, picnic tables, state park fee campsites

Size: Large

Overnight parking: Allowed. Permit required. Please check in with state park staff.

Winter access: The main trailhead is unplowed, but a small parking area is typically plowed near the state park contact station.

Special notes: State park permit required for day use and overnight parking. Day use parking is available at Southern Camp 20 Road Trailhead. At MN-61 milepost 124.4, turn north on North Rd., go 2.75 miles. Turn north on Camp 20 Rd., go 1.8 miles to a pull-off on side of Camp 20 Rd. GPS: 47.866692, -90.047911

SECTION SNAPSHOT

Trail Atlas maps: F-4, F-5

Total distance: 6.3 miles

Elevation change: Significant elevation change down to and up from the Brule River

SHT campsites: None. Plan your mileage accordingly; this is the longest stretch without campsites north of the City of Duluth.

Hazards and concerns: Many stairs between the trailhead and Devil's Kettle. This section has the longest roadwalk on the Trail. Though rural, it does see truck traffic.

Synopsis: The most mysterious waterfall of the North Shore is showcased in this section. The Trail visits Devil's Kettle and continues along the Brule River, climbing to Bald Hill Vista before traversing the longest roadwalk on the Superior Hiking Trail.

Pro tip: From Judge C.R. Magney State Park heading north, the SHT takes on a more rugged, wild feel. Cell reception may be unreliable.

MILEAGE	Northbound	Southbound
Judge C.R. Magney State Park Trailhead	**0.0**	**6.3**
Brule River bridge	0.1	6.2
Too many stairs	0.8	5.5
Devil's Kettle	1.0	5.3
Bald Hill Vista	3.9	2.4
Flute Reed River bridge	4.5	1.8
Southern Camp 20 Road Trailhead, south end roadwalk	4.6	1.7
North end roadwalk	6.3	0.0
Northern Camp 20 Road Trailhead	**6.3**	**0.0**

The Hovland Gap Story

The Superior Hiking Trail north of Judge C.R. Magney State Park offers exceptionally challenging trail experiences. Given its remote, rugged nature, it was one of the toughest places to find a route for the Trail. It's no surprise that for many years, the Trail north of Judge C.R. Magney State Park barely existed. Much of the route was composed of dead-end trail segments and miles and miles of roadwalk. This area was known as the Hovland Gap.

It took years of effort to close the Hovland Gap by finding suitable terrain for the Superior Hiking Trail and securing permissions from many private landowners in the area. Eventually in the early 2000s, the Trail found its home on the route we know today.

A piece of the Hovland Gap still exists—it's the 1.7-mile dirt roadwalk connecting the northern and southern Camp 20 Road trailheads. And just like the trailbuilders of the past, the Superior Hiking Trail Association is still aspiring to someday close the last substantial gap along the trail corridor. ⋀⋀

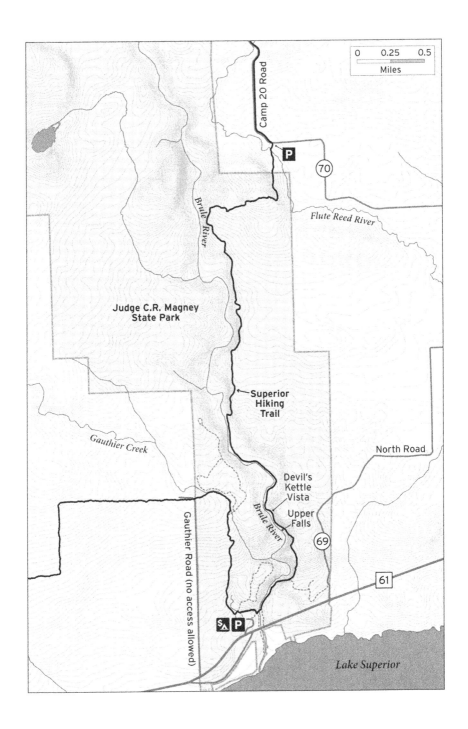

Northern Camp 20 Road Trailhead to Arrowhead Trail Trailhead

BEGINNING TRAILHEAD

Directions and GPS Waypoints: At MN-61 milepost 124.4, turn north on North Rd. and go 2.75 miles. Turn north on Camp 20 Rd. and go 4.75 miles to parking lot on right. GPS: 47.884791, -90.061140

Facilities: None

Size: Small

Overnight parking: Allowed

Winter access: No

Special notes: Trailhead was for many years called the Cook County Road 70 Trailhead, but its more accurate, current name is Northern Camp 20 Road Trailhead.

SECTION SNAPSHOT

Trail Atlas maps: F-5, F-6

Total distance: 7.9 miles (Additional 400-foot spur trail to Arrowhead Trail Trailhead)

Elevation change: With the exception of a couple of noteworthy, steep climbs, this section is predominantly gentle and rolling.

SHT campsites: Three

Hazards and concerns: There may be short, flooded areas in this section, most likely on Tom Lake Road.

Synopsis: The Trail meanders through forests in various stages of regrowth, shares Tom Lake Road (a wide, little-used multi-use trail), then ascends to pretty beaver ponds.

Pro tip: This area is among the moosiest sections of the Trail. While you may not see one, they are likely to have left a trace of their presence.

▮ **Arrowhead Trail Trailhead.** A 400-foot spur trail crosses a bridge over Carlson Creek and climbs quickly to the Arrowhead Trail Trailhead.

CAMPSITES

▲ **Hazel Campsite**

Size: Small

Water source: None. Water might be found 0.3 miles north at a small, unreliable stream. Northbound hikers should plan to carry water from one of the Flute Reed River tributary crossings, approximately 2.0 miles south.

Due to the long distance between the Little Brule River campsites and Hazel Campsite, this site often fills up. Those who are able should plan to camp at South Carlson Pond Campsite or North Carlson Pond Campsite to avoid overuse of this campsite.

11.7, 11.7 ⊕ ⊕ 2.8, 4.9

▲ **South Carlson Pond Campsite**

Size: Medium

Water source: A large beaver pond

Campsite is located on a small, piney hill above the pond. Users have reported difficulties hanging food bags at this campsite.

14.5, 2.8 ⊕ ⊕ 2.1, 5.8

▲ **North Carlson Pond Campsite**

Size: Medium

Water source: A small beaver pond

Campsite is located in the forest above the pond.

4.9, 2.1 ⊕ ⊕ 3.7, 7.0

MILEAGE	Northbound	Southbound
Northern Camp 20 Road Trailhead	**0.0**	**7.9**
Hazel Campsite	2.1	5.8
Tom Lake Road roadwalk west end	2.4	5.5
Optional rugged trail around flooded area	3.6	4.3
Tom Lake Road roadwalk east end	3.8	4.1
Carlson Creek crossing	4.8	3.1
South Carlson Pond Campsite	4.9	3.0
Arrowhead Trail crossing	6.6	1.3
North Carlson Pond Campsite	7.0	0.9
Spur to Arrowhead Trail Trailhead	*7.9*	*0.0*
Arrowhead Trail Trailhead	**7.9**	**0.0**

Arrowhead Trail Trailhead to Jackson Lake Road Trailhead

Directions and GPS Waypoints: At MN-61 milepost 128.9, turn north on Arrowhead Trail, go 3.3 miles to parking lot on right. GPS: 47.887656, -89.952394

Facilities: None

Size: Medium

Overnight parking: Allowed

Winter access: No

Special notes: Please park within the trailhead and not along the road to avoid blocking logging trucks and other traffic on Arrowhead Trail.

SECTION SNAPSHOT

Trail Atlas map: F-6

Total distance: 4.7 miles (Additional 400-foot spur from Arrowhead Trail Trailhead, 350-foot spur to Jackson Lake Road Trailhead)

Elevation change: Significant, with a long ridge walk

SHT campsites: One

Hazards and concerns: Steep, rocky terrain and cliff edges

Synopsis: Trail climbs to one of the longest and most dramatic ridgelines of the Superior Hiking Trail featuring stunning views, including Hellacious Overlook.

Pro tip: For those who enjoy biking on dirt roads, this section is a great one to self-shuttle between trailheads.

SPUR TRAIL

- **Arrowhead Trail Trailhead.** A 400-foot spur trail drops dramatically to a bridge over Carlson Creek and the junction with the main SHT.

- **Jackson Lake Road Trailhead.** Parking area is located 350 feet north of the trail crossing on Jackson Lake Road. Follow the minimally-traveled, dirt Jackson Lake Road.

CAMPSITES

▲ **Caribou Pond Campsite**
Size: Small
Water source is from an adjacent beaver pond which fluctuates wildly in size.
Campsite is near a recent timber harvest area.
5.8, 3.7 ⬅ ➔ 3.3, 8.4

MILEAGE	Northbound	Southbound
Arrowhead Trail Trailhead	*0.0*	*4.7*
Spur from Arrowhead Trail Trailhead	*0.0*	*4.7*
Pond	1.3	3.4
Caribou Pond Campsite	2.8	1.9
Hellacious Overlook	3.5	1.2
Jackson Lake Road crossing or roadwalk east to Jackson Lake Road Trailhead.	*4.7*	*0.0*
Jackson Lake Road Trailhead	*4.7*	*0.0*

Jackson Lake Road Trailhead to Andy Lake Road Trailhead

Directions and GPS Waypoints: At MN-61 milepost 128.9, turn north on Arrowhead Trail, go 4.5 miles. Turn east on Jackson Lake Rd., go 3.1 miles to parking lot on left. GPS: 47.913831, -89.897988

Facilities: None

Size: Small

Overnight parking: Allowed

Winter access: No

Special notes: Jackson Lake Road is typically unplowed in the winter.

SECTION SNAPSHOT

Trail Atlas maps: F-6, F-7

Total distance: 4.9 miles (Additional 350-foot spur trail from Jackson Lake Road Trailhead)

Elevation change: There is substantial elevation change on this section, though much of it is fairly gentle.

SHT campsites: One

Hazards and concerns: Many rocks and some steep areas

Synopsis: Trail explores a cedar swamp on an impressively long and simple boardwalk, winds past a large glacial erratic, and climbs to the highest point of the Superior Hiking Trail at Rosebush Ridge.

Pro tip: Don't be discouraged by the lack of a view at Rosebush Ridge—there's a vista just a mile north.

SPUR TRAIL

■ **Jackson Lake Road Trailhead.** Parking area is located 350 feet north of the trail crossing on Jackson Lake Road. Follow the minimally-traveled, dirt Jackson Lake Road.

▲ **Jackson Creek Campsite**
Size: Small
Water source: Jackson Creek, located just north of the campsite. In dry conditions, follow the creek north to some shallow pools.
Campsite is small and notoriously rocky and rooty.
7.0, 3.3 ⊕ ⊕ 5.1

MILEAGE	Northbound	Southbound
Jackson Lake Road Trailhead	**0.0**	**4.9**
Roadwalk from Jackson Lake Road Trailhead	*0.0*	*4.9*
Jackson Creek Campsite	1.4	3.5
Rosebush Ridge, highest elevation of SHT at 1829 ft.	3.6	1.3
Vista, bench	4.6	0.3
Andy Lake Road Trailhead, crossing	**4.9**	**0.0**

▌ Andy Lake Road Trailhead to Otter Lake Road Trailhead

BEGINNING TRAILHEAD

Directions and GPS Waypoints: At MN-61 milepost 128.9, turn north on Arrowhead Trail, go 4.5 miles. Turn east on Jackson Lake Rd., go 6.2 miles to turn west on Andy Lake Rd. Go 1.6 miles on Andy Lake Rd. to parking lot on right. GPS: 47.951281, -89.919507

Facilities: None

Size: Medium

Overnight parking: Allowed

Winter access: No

Special notes: Andy Lake Road is unplowed in the winter. It is a narrow road with little to no room to pull off when another car is coming. Due to these factors, use this trailhead with caution.

SECTION SNAPSHOT

Trail Atlas map: F-7

Total distance: 3.3 miles

Elevation change: Minimal

SHT campsites: One

Hazards and concerns: Frequent logging in this area may obscure the route at times.

Synopsis: This extremely remote section is one of the flattest, often following logging roads.

Pro tip: A low-lying, brushy area near the aptly-named Swamp River boasts one of the best ecosystems for seeing small mammals and mosquitoes.

▲ **Andy Creek Campsite**

Size: Small

Water source: Andy Creek, just north of the campsite

Remote area is great for wildlife viewing and listening. Users have reported difficulties hanging food bags and hammocks at this campsite.

8.4, 5.1 ⊖

MILEAGE	Northbound	Southbound
Andy Lake Road Trailhead	**0.0**	**3.3**
Andy Creek Campsite	1.6	1.7
Andy Creek bridge	1.6	1.7
Logging road south end	2.6	0.7
Logging road north end	3.3	0.0
Otter Lake Road Trailhead, register	**3.3**	**0.0**

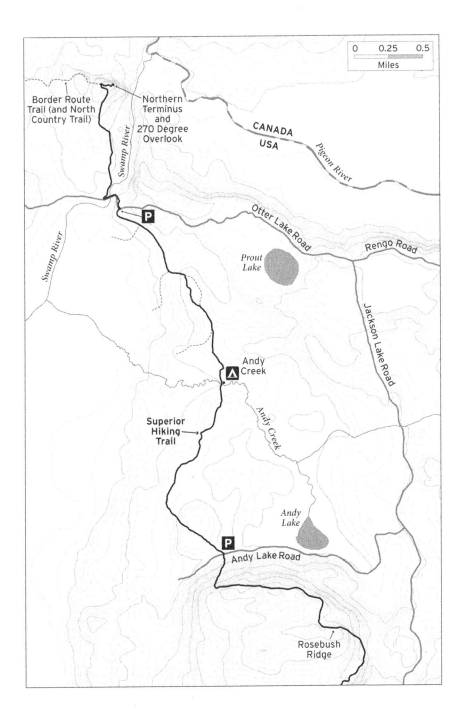

■ Otter Lake Road to Northern Terminus

Directions and GPS Waypoints: Otter Lake Road Trailhead. At MN-61 milepost 128.9, turn north on Arrowhead Trail, go 4.5 miles. Turn east on Jackson Lake Rd., go 8.4 miles. Turn west on Otter Lake Rd. Go 2.0 miles to parking lot on left. GPS: 47.986537, -89.933372

Facilities: Trail register

Size: Medium

Overnight parking: Allowed

Winter access: No

Special notes: Otter Lake Road is unplowed in the winter and often impassable in the spring until road conditions dry out. For long-term parking, please use the Superior Hiking Trail Trailhead and leave the nearby Border Route Trail Trailhead (Continue on Otter Lake Road 0.2 miles to Border Route Trail parking lot on right. GPS: 47.987672, -89.935896) for BRT users.

SECTION SNAPSHOT

Trail Atlas map: F-7

Total distance: 1.2 miles one-way (2.4 miles as an out-and-back hike)

Elevation change: It is a steady climb to the northern terminus.

SHT campsites: None

Hazards and concerns: Rocky drop-offs at the northern terminus

Synopsis: The first or final mile of the Superior Hiking Trail climbs to the stunning 270 Degree Overlook and its trail register, where trail users can share their memories or aspirations.

Pro tip: Most cell reception at the northern terminus originates in Canada, which is in a different time zone than Minnesota.

MILEAGE	Northbound	Southbound
Otter Lake Road Trailhead, register	**0.0**	**1.2**
Otter Lake Road roadwalk east end	0.0	1.2
Otter Lake Road roadwalk west end, Border Route Trail parking lot	0.2	1.0
Border Route Trail south end	0.2	1.0
Border Route Trail north end	1.1	0.1
270 Degree Overlook, Superior Hiking Trail northern terminus, register	1.2	0.0

Campsite Distance Index

| CAMPSITE NAME | DISTANCE TO NEXT CAMPSITE | | SIZE |
	Northbound	Southbound	
Red River Valley Campsite	53.1	N/A	Medium
Bald Eagle Campsite	1.2	53.1	Small
White Pine Campsite	5.5	1.2	Medium
Lone Tree Campsite	3.7	5.5	Small
Heron Pond Campsite	4.0	3.7	Medium
Sucker River Campsite	2.7	4.0	Medium
Fox Farm Pond Campsite	7.3	2.7	Medium
Big Bend Campsite	6.1	7.3	Medium
McCarthy Creek Campsite	1.1	6.1	Small
Ferguson Campsite	5.5	1.1	Small
Stewart River Campsite	4.0	5.5	Medium
Reeves Falls Campsite	5.7	4.0	Small
Silver Creek Campsite	8.4	5.7	Medium
Crow Valley Campsite	3.2	8.4	Medium
West Gooseberry Campsite	0.9	3.2	Medium
East Gooseberry Campsite	0.1	0.9	Small
Middle Gooseberry Campsite	0.8	0.1	Small
Gooseberry Multigroup Campsite	6.2	0.8	Large
Blueberry Hill Campsite	3.9	6.2	Medium

CAMPSITE NAME	DISTANCE TO NEXT CAMPSITE		SIZE
	Northbound	Southbound	
SW Split Rock River Campsite	0.3	3.9	Medium
NW Split Rock River Campsite	0.2	0.3	Medium
NE Split Rock River Campsite	0.3	0.2	Large
SE Split Rock River Campsite	4.6	0.3	Small
Chapins Ridge Campsite	1.7	4.6	Medium
Beaver Pond Campsite	1.4	1.7	Medium
Fault Line Creek Campsite	4.4	1.4	Medium
West Beaver River Campsite	0.3	4.4	Small
East Beaver River Campsite	5.3	0.3	Small
Penn Creek Campsite	1.2	5.3	Large
Bear Lake Campsite	1.2	1.2	Small
Round Mountain Campsite	0.5	1.2	Medium
West Palisade Campsite	0.1	0.5	Medium
East Palisade Campsite	8.0	0.1	Large
West Kennedy Campsite	0.0	8.0	Medium
East Kennedy Campsite	6.1	0.0	Medium
Section 13 Campsite	3.7	6.1	Medium
Leskinen Creek Campsite	4.6	3.7	Medium
South Egge Lake Campsite	0.2	4.6	Medium
North Egge Lake Campsite	3.0	0.2	Medium
South Sonju Lake Campsite	0.3	3.0	Large
North Sonju Lake Campsite	1.8	0.3	Medium
East Branch Baptism River Campsite	0.6	1.8	Small
Blesner Creek Campsite	2.0	0.6	Small
Aspen Knob Campsite	5.0	2.0	Small
Horseshoe Ridge Campsite	2.8	5.0	Medium
West Caribou Campsite	0.1	2.8	Small
East Caribou Campsite	1.4	0.1	Large
Crystal Creek Campsite	2.6	1.4	Medium
Sugarloaf Pond Campsite	3.4	2.6	Medium
Dyers Creek Campsite	2.9	3.4	Medium

CAMPSITE NAME	DISTANCE TO NEXT CAMPSITE		SIZE
	Northbound	Southbound	
Fredenberg Creek Campsite	1.8	2.9	Large
The Falls Campsite	0.8	1.8	Small
The Ledge Campsite	0.6	0.8	Small
North Cross River Campsite	0.1	0.6	Small
South Cross River Campsite	8.9	0.1	Medium
Springdale Creek Campsite	2.2	8.9	Medium
West Leveaux Campsite	0.1	2.2	Medium
East Leveaux Campsite	1.2	0.1	Small
Onion River Campsite	2.0	1.2	Large
West Rollins Creek Campsite	0.0	2.0	Medium
East Rollins Creek Campsite	4.4	0.0	Small
Mystery Mountain Campsite	2.1	4.4	Large
West Poplar Campsite	0.4	2.1	Medium
East Poplar Campsite	2.9	0.4	Small
West Lake Agnes Campsite	0.4	2.9	Medium
East Lake Agnes Campsite	2.3	0.4	Medium
Jonvick Creek Campsite	2.2	2.3	Small
Spruce Creek Campsite	3.2	2.2	Large
Camp Creek Campsite	3.0	3.2	Large
Big White Pine Campsite	0.5	3.0	Small
Cut Log Campsite	2.4	0.5	Small
Trout Creek Campsite			Large
North Cascade River Campsite	4.0	2.4	Large
Sundling Creek Campsite	1.7	4.0	Medium
South Bally Creek Pond Campsite	0.2	1.7	Medium
North Bally Creek Pond Campsite	10.6	0.2	Small
West Devil Track Campsite	0.1	10.6	Large
East Devil Track Campsite	2.5	0.1	Small
Woods Creek Campsite	2.4	2.5	Medium
Durfee Creek Campsite	1.1	2.4	Large
Cliff Creek Campsite	2.5	1.1	Large

| CAMPSITE NAME | DISTANCE TO NEXT CAMPSITE | | SIZE |
	Northbound	Southbound	
Kimball Creek Campsite	1.2	2.5	Small
Crow Creek Campsite	0.3	1.2	Medium
West Fork Kadunce Campsite	0.5	0.3	Medium
Kadunce River Campsite	5.2	0.5	Small
South Little Brule River Campsite	0.4	5.2	Small
North Little Brule Campsite	0.0	0.4	Medium
Northwest Little Brule River Campsite	11.7	0.0	Small
Hazel Campsite	2.8	11.7	Small
South Carlson Pond Campsite	2.1	2.8	Medium
North Carlson Pond Campsite	3.7	2.1	Medium
Caribou Pond Campsite	3.3	3.7	Small
Jackson Creek Campsite	5.1	3.3	Small
Andy Creek Campsite	N/A	5.1	Small

Trailhead Index

TRAILHEAD NAME	Overnight Parking Allowed	Winter Access
Wild Valley Road Trailhead	●	
Jay Cooke State Park Trailhead	With park permit	●
Grand Portage Trailhead		●
131st Avenue W. Trailhead		
123rd Avenue W. Trailhead		●
Magney Snively Trailhead		●
Spirit Mountain Grand Avenue Chalet Trailhead		●
Spirit Mountain Parking Lot D		●
Waseca Street Trailhead		
Skyline Parkway Trailhead		
Haines Road Trailhead		
N. 24th Avenue W. Trailhead		
Twin Ponds Trailhead		●
Rose Garden Trailhead		●
Hartley Nature Center Trailhead		●
Martin Road Trailhead	●	●
Lismore Road*		
Normanna Road Trailhead	●	●
Western Fox Farm Road Trailhead	●	

TRAILHEAD NAME	Overnight Parking Allowed	Winter Access
Eastern Fox Farm Road Trailhead	●	●
Rossini Road Trailhead	●	
Lake County Demonstration Forest Trailhead	●	●
Reeves Road Trailhead	●	
Lake County Road 301 Trailhead	●	●
W. Castle Danger Road Trailhead	●	
Gooseberry Falls State Park Visitor Center Trailhead		●
Split Rock River Wayside Trailhead		●
Cove Point Lodge Trailhead	●	●
Lax Lake Road Trailhead	●	●
Penn Boulevard Trailhead	●	●
Bay Area Historical Society Trailhead	●	
Highway 1 Trailhead	●	
Lake County Road 6 Trailhead	●	
Lake County Road 7 Trailhead	●	●
Sonju Lake Road Trailhead	●	
George Crosby Manitou State Park Trailhead	With park permit	●
Caribou Falls State Wayside Trailhead		
Sugarloaf Road Trailhead	●	
Cook County Road 1 Trailhead	●	
Skou Road Trailhead	●	
Temperance River Road Trailhead	●	
Temperance River Wayside Trailhead		●
Sawbill Trail Trailhead	●	●
Onion River Road Trailhead	●	●
Ski Hill Road Trailhead	●	●
Caribou Trail Trailhead	●	
Cascade River Wayside		●
Cook County Road 45 Trailhead	●	
Sundling Creek Trailhead	●	●

TRAILHEAD NAME	Overnight Parking Allowed	Winter Access
Bally Creek Road Trailhead	●	●
Cook County Road 6 Trailhead	●	●
Pincushion Mountain Trailhead	●	●
Lindskog Road Trailhead	●	
Cook County Road 14 Trailhead	●	
Kadunce River Wayside Trailhead		●
Judge C.R. Magney State Park Trailhead	With park permit	Nearby*
Southern Camp 20 Road Trailhead		
Northern Camp 20 Road Trailhead	●	
Arrowhead Trail Trailhead	●	
Jackson Lake Road	●	
Andy Lake Road Trailhead	●	
Otter Lake Road Trailhead	●	

Overnight parking is also available within state parks. Check in with park staff for location of overnight parking lot. A state park pass is required.

Plowing of trailheads may not be consistent. Some roads, primarily in the vicinity of Arrowhead Trail, are unplowed during winter. Check the Trail Conditions page for updates.

*Main parking lot unplowed, but day use parking available near office.

Acknowledgments

SPECIAL THANKS

• Denny Caneff (SHTA Executive Director, 2017-2020) for his efforts to launch this guidebook revision.

• Maddie Cohen (maddiecohen.com) for her detailed proofreading services.

• Matt Kania (Map Hero Inc.) for crafting beautiful maps for this publication.

• Sally Rauschenfels (Sally Rauschenfels Creative) for her exceptional graphic design and overall project guidance.

DATA ACKNOWLEDGMENTS

• GPS and mile point data was originally collected by GeoPOI LLC in September and October 2018, with updates provided by the SHTA.

• Trail data processed by Melody Morris, SHTA GIS Intern.

SHTA Project Coordination by: Jaron Cramer, Lisa Luokkala, and Jo Swanson.

This guidebook was prepared by the Superior Hiking Trail Association using Federal funds under award NA19NOS4190063 from the Coastal Zone Management Act of 1972, as amended, administered by the Office for Coastal Management, National Oceanic and Atmospheric Administration (NOAA), U.S. Department of Commerce provided to the Minnesota Department of Natural Resources (MNDNR) for Minnesota's Lake Superior Coastal Program. The statements, findings, conclusions, and recommendations are those of the authors and do not necessarily reflect the views of NOAA, the U.S. Department of Commerce, or the MNDNR.

DEPARTMENT OF NATURAL RESOURCES